Navigating the Ecological Transition

The transition towards sustainability is now a major issue that has taken centre stage in public debate, policy circles, scientific forums, and business roundtables. Higher education institutions focusing on educating tomorrow's managers and leaders and on business practices are doubly challenged by this development. On the one hand, they must be accountable to their internal stakeholders who strongly identify with the new "environmental awakening". On the other hand, because of their status as research institutions, they must provide answers and propose solutions to face this challenge which is shaping up to be the most crucial issue that humanity has had to face in the modern era.

In this book, faculty and researchers from *École Supérieure de Sciences Économiques et Commerciales* (ESSEC Business School), a recognized leader among European schools of business and management, provide a multi-faceted perspective on the different areas that need to be considered to understand the new market dynamics during this environmental and social transition. The book identifies the obstacles that come in the way of the transformation of dominant business models, and how to overcome them in order to move away from "business as usual". The various chapters in this work offer a vast diversity of approaches that address the paradigm shift towards sustainability, providing insights for both business and higher education. The book includes chapters from seven different departments at ESSEC: Management; Accounting and Management Control; Economics; Information Systems; Decision Sciences and Statistics; Marketing; Operations Management; and Public and Private Policy.

Research-based and combining theory with practice, this thought-provoking book will be welcomed by academics, institutions, and professionals alike, wishing to gain perspectives on the challenges of the transition towards a sustainable society.

Hugues Bouthinon-Dumas is Associate Professor of Law in the Public and Private Policy department and the Head of the Public Affairs Track at ESSEC Business School in Paris. He holds a doctorate in economic law from Paris Dauphine University and his "Habilitation" from Paris Sorbonne University. He teaches business law, legal aspects of the ecological transition, sustainable finance, company law, and economic criminal law. He is also a part-time judge at the Nanterre court (Paris Business District). His interest areas cover markets regulation, company law, including corporate governance issues, Law and Management, and legal theory.

Arijit Chatterjee is Professor of Management and Academic Director of the Asian Strategy Consulting Project at ESSEC Business School. His research interests are in strategic decision-making, how inequality within and outside of firms is addressed through institutional mechanisms and social movements, how challengers and incumbents use disruptive tactics in strategic action fields, and how small organizations can address grand challenges.

Bernard Leca is Professor of Management Control, Chaired Professor on Ecological Transition at ESSEC Business School, and Academic Director of the *Evaluation et Mesure d'Impact Social et Environnemental* (EMISE) Laboratory. He researches and works with companies and other organizations on topics related to sustainability. He focuses on sustainable development goals, and issues related to climate change and biodiversity collapse with a particular focus on power asymmetry among actors, and how this might influence adaptation and mitigation processes.

Routledge Advances in Management and Business Studies

Entrepreneurship Education and Internationalisation
Cases, Collaborations and Contexts
Edited by Robert James Crammond and Denis Hyams-Ssekasi

Sustainable Business in the Era of Digital Transformation
Strategic and Entrepreneurial Perspectives
Mariusz Sołtysik, Magdalena Wojnarowska, Maria Urbaniec, Vesna Zabkar, Marek Ćwiklicki and Erica Varese

How to Manage and Survive during a Global Crisis
Lessons for Managers from the COVID-19 Pandemic
Piyush Sharma and Tak Yan Leung

Understanding Procrastination at Work
Individual and Workplace Perspectives
Beata Bajcar

Entrepreneurship in the BRICS
Economic Development and Growth in the Post-Pandemic World
Edited by Ndivhuho Tshikovhi, Fulufhelo Netswera and Ravinder Rena

Start-up Strategy and Entrepreneurial Development
Evolving Business Models and Economic Trends
Edited by Iwona Skalna and Aleksandra Gąsior

Enterprise Risk Management
Technical, Cognitive, and Social Perspectives
Mirna Jabbour and Jason Crawford

Navigating the Ecological Transition
A Business School Perspective
Edited by Hugues Bouthinon-Dumas, Arijit Chatterjee and Bernard Leca

For more information about this series, please visit: www.routledge.com/Routledge-Advances-in-Management-and-Business-Studies/book-series/SE0305

Navigating the Ecological Transition

A Business School Perspective

Edited by Hugues Bouthinon-Dumas, Arijit Chatterjee and Bernard Leca

Routledge
Taylor & Francis Group
LONDON AND NEW YORK

First published 2025
by Routledge
4 Park Square, Milton Park, Abingdon, Oxon OX14 4RN

and by Routledge
605 Third Avenue, New York, NY 10158

Routledge is an imprint of the Taylor & Francis Group, an informa business

British Library Cataloguing-in-Publication Data
A catalogue record for this book is available from the British Library

ISBN: 978-1-032-82461-1 (hbk)
ISBN: 978-1-032-86318-4 (pbk)
ISBN: 978-1-003-52235-5 (ebk)

DOI: 10.4324/9781003522355

Typeset in Sabon LT Pro
by Apex CoVantage

Contents

Contributors

Hamid Bouchikhi is a professor and chair of the department of management at ESSEC Business School. His research interests are in managerial innovation, organizational identity and entrepreneurship. He received the prize for the best research in SME management (France, 2009) and for the best professor of Organizational Behavior (World Human Resources Congress, Mumbai, 2011). In 2014, the MIT Sloan Management Review awarded him the Richard Beckhard Memorial Prize for an article on identity integration in mergers and acquisitions. In 2021, Thinkers 50 named him among the '30 influential management thinkers'. He has taught at Keio University in Tokyo and at University Putra Malaysia in Kuala Lumpur. Hamid was Dean of SolBridge International School of Business (South Korea) and member of the Special Commission on the Development Model (CSMD) appointed by the King of Morocco.

Fabrice Cavarretta is Associate Professor at ESSEC Business School, whose research focuses on managerial doctrines with substantive applications in leadership, intrapreneurship, and ecological transition. He teaches leadership and intrapreneurship. Previously, he worked in Silicon Valley and served as a division director at a major media/telecom. Holder of a PhD in management sciences from INSEAD, Fabrice Cavarretta has studied at the Santa Fe Institute, Harvard Business School, and Ecole Polytechnique. His next book coauthored with environmental activist Eric Lenoir explores our relationship to both ecological and social ecosystems (Payot, 2024).

Mark Christensen is Professor of Accounting and Management Control at ESSEC Business School (Singapore). He researches accounting as a socio-technical construction with publications involving public sector performance reporting; consultants; accrual accounting; accounting history; animal welfare; audit as a blame instrument; and related topics. His work appears in journals such as *Accounting, Auditing & Accountability Journal*; *Accounting, Organizations & Society*; *Accounting Education*; *Accounting History*; *Australian Accounting Review*; *Comptabilité Contrôle Audit*; *Contemporary Accounting Research*; *Critical Perspectives on Accounting*; *European Accounting Review*; *International Review of Administrative Sciences*; *Journal* *of Business Ethics*; *Financial Accountability & Management*; *Management Accounting Research*; and *Public Money & Management*.

Cristina Davino is Associate Professor of Statistics at the University of Naples Federico II, Italy. Her fields of interest and areas of expertise are multidimensional data analysis, data mining, quantile regression, statistical surveys, quality of life assessment, evaluation of university education processes, construction and validation of composite indicators, and analysis of learning processes. She has been involved in many research projects whose results have been disseminated in international journals and conferences.

Viviane de Beaufort is Professor at ESSEC Business School, Director of the European Center Law and Economics (CEDE), and Founder and Director of Women ESSEC Exec programmes. A former Jean Monnet chair (2023–2026), she is the author of numerous publications and conferences on corporate governance and company law, international trade, lobbying, and European public policies. Viviane is a member of think tanks (Europe/Gender issues), board member, and adviser of public and private entities, including the European Union. She has experimented in management, strategy, entrepreneurship, and international issues and is deeply involved in gender issues as referent at ESSEC.

Laurence de Carlo is Professor at ESSEC Business School and has been associated with the ESSEC Urban Economic Chair since 1994. She was first trained in civil engineering and urban planning at *Institut National des Sciences Appliquées de Lyon* (INSA Lyon) and holds a PhD degree in urban and regional planning from the University of Montréal. She conducts research and has published in the areas of participation of the public and stakeholders in planning and environment decision processes and of energy transition stakes and their teaching. In 2022, she represented ESSEC in the multi-stakeholders' initiative coordinated by The Shift Project NGO regarding the teaching of ecological transition in management schools.

Marie-Léandre Gomez is Associate Professor in Management Control at ESSEC Business school. Her research focuses on the dynamics of organizational activity: organizational learning, the coordination of inter-professional teams, and the role of financial and non-financial tools in managerial and professional practices. She has studied these phenomena in professional organizations, including three-star restaurants, police SWAT forces, and hospitals. Her work is based on processual and practical approaches on organizations.

Stefan Gröschl is Professor in the Department of Management. He is known for his expertise in responsible leadership, sustainable business practices, diversity and inclusion, and international human resources management. His research has been published in textbooks, book chapters, and articles in both the international trade and academic press. He is an editorial board member and reviewer for international academic management journals. Stefan has conducted company training programmes and consultancies for firms in France and abroad. Stefan has served as an external examiner to various governmental programmes in Europe and North America.

Geneviève Helleringer holds a JD from Columbia University (1999), an MSc in legal sociology from Paris II Panthéon Assas University (2009), and an MSc and a doctorate in private law from the Sorbonne University (2010) (receiving four national prizes for her doctoral thesis). She is a member of the Law Faculty, the deputy director of the Institute of European and Comparative Law, and a research fellow at Lady Margaret Hall. She is also Law Professor at ESSEC Business School and an appointed research member of the European Corporate Governance Institute (ECGI). Her research focuses on comparative contract, corporate and financial law, and commercial dispute resolution.

Geoffrey Lamberton, PhD, is Senior Lecturer in the Faculty of Business, Law and Arts at Southern Cross University, Australia. His research interests include sustainability in accounting and business; the international student experience; intercultural learning; critical accounting; and business ethics. He has published in journals such as *Journal of Business Ethics*; *Critical Perspectives on Accounting*; *Sustainability*; *Sustainable Development*; *Journal of Research in International Education*; *Journal of Management & Organisation*; and *Accounting Forum*.

Emmanuelle Le Nagard is Professor of Marketing at ESSEC Business School and is currently Academic Director of the Master in Management. Her research expertise includes marketing strategy, ethics in marketing, and marketing of innovations, especially consumer innovations and diffusion of innovations. She has published articles in *International Journal of Research in Marketing*, *Journal of Product Innovation Management*, *Research and Applications in Marketing*, and *Journal of Cleaner Production*, among others. She is particularly interested in the evolution of marketing facing the environmental and social world challenges.

Marion Ligonie got her PhD in management sciences from ESSEC Business School in 2016 and is now an associate professor in management control at *Institut d'Économie Scientifique Et de Gestion* (IESEG School of Management). She is interested in management control practices as sociological phenomena, particularly in relation to sustainability. Her research examines how sustainability tools affect managers' new and existing activities. More specifically, Marion is interested in how nature is translated into financial language and integrated into organizational practices and decision-making. She uses in-depth qualitative methods such as ethnography and case studies.

Cédomir Nestorovic holds a PhD from the Institute of Political Science in Paris (Sciences Po) and is currently Professor of Geopolitics and Islamic Business at ESSEC Business School. He is Founder and Academic Director of the ESSEC & Mannheim Executive MBA Asia-Pacific and of the MBA programme at the Arabian Gulf University, Manama, Bahrain. He was awarded the title of "Professor of the Week" by the *Financial Times* in 2012 and the best teacher prize at ESSEC in 2017. Professor Nestorovic is the author of the book *Geopolitics and Business, Relevance and Resonance*, published by Springer in 2023.

Xavier Pavie is Professor at ESSEC Business School, programme director at the Collège International de Philosophie, and research associate at the Institute of Philosophical Research at Paris Nanterre University. He is the founder of the iMagination Center and the author of around 20 books dedicated to philosophical spiritual exercises, which he applies to aspects of lifestyle, responsibility, innovation, and imagination. His book *Toward Responsible Innovation* (PUF 2018) was voted the best management book of 2019 by *Fondation Nationale pour l'Enseignement de la Gestion des Entreprises* (FNEGE). Xavier has been recognized as one of LinkedIn Top Voices (No. 5) in the Education category.

Estefania Santacreu-Vasut is Professor of Economics at ESSEC Business School and *Théorie économique, modélisation et applications* (THEMA) and an associate dean for pedagogy. She obtained her PhD in economics from UC Berkeley in 2010. Her research focuses on gender and institutions and has been published in outlets such as the *Journal of Development Economics*, *Journal of Economic Behavior and Organization*, among others. She is a consultant for the OECD, has advised the EU on its gender equality strategy, and is a co-founder of the project Gender & Finance and the co-author, together with Tom Gamble, of the popular press book *The Nature of Goods and the Goods of Nature: Why Anti-Globalization Is Not the Answer*.

Vincenzo Esposito Vinzi has been Dean and President of ESSEC Business School since January 2018. He holds a doctorate in computational statistics from the University of Naples Federico II and has been a visiting professor and lecturer at several universities throughout the world. In 2007, he joined ESSEC as a professor of statistics and was elected Dean of Faculty in December 2011. He sits on several Boards of Directors and International Advisory Boards. He is also a member of the OECD Business for Inclusive Growth partnership. He is President of the Diversity Commission of the *Conférence des Grandes Écoles* (CGE).

Radu Vranceanu is Professor of Economics at ESSEC Business School and a research fellow with CNRS THEMA (National Centre for Scientific Research). He holds a doctorate in economics from the University of Paris II, *Habilitation à Diriger des Recherches* (HDR), and is widely recognized as having special expertise in the theory of expectations and the analysis of informational inefficiencies, which he has applied to various fields, including financial and exchange rate crises, monetary and public debt policies, research management, defence economics, labour contracts, health economics, and managerial behaviour. He is also a contributor to research in experimental economics at ESSEC, with studies in team production, lies and deception, negotiation, and coordination games. In 2000–2001, Radu Vranceanu worked for the UN Economic Commission for Europe; he also served as Dean for Research of ESSEC Business School for many years. Since 2020, he has been the ESSEC representative for scientific integrity (RIS).

Adrian Zicari is Teaching Professor in the Accounting and Management Control Department of ESSEC Business School, Paris. He is Academic Director of the Council on Business & Society, an international alliance of 11 business schools. His work appears in several journals, including *Critical Perspectives in Accounting*, *Journal of Business Ethics*, *Journal of Cleaner Production*, and *Social and Environmental Accountability Journal*, among others. He is Associate Editor for Issues in *Accounting Education*, the pedagogical journal of the American Accounting Association. He is Editor in the Routledge CoBS Focus on Responsible Business. He is also an honorary representative of Buenos Aires City in Paris and a Guardian for the Global Responsible Leadership Initiative (GRLI).

Preface

Ecological transition is increasingly shaping debates on the evolution of the economy, the role of business in society, and the policies that should regulate the economic system. This challenge is of a completely different nature to the opposing ideologies since the 1930s between liberal democracies and authoritarian regimes characterized by central planning. The problem of developing the economies of non-industrialized countries, particularly after post-war decolonization, was also completely different. Meanwhile, humans have altered the status of the planet. Formerly the battlefield—or the geographical framework—for economic activity, it has become an interest that must be protected for the good of all human beings. The great economic debate is no longer between East and West, or North and South, but between a planet that is habitable for human beings and a mortifying unconsciousness. This new challenge is now at the forefront of public debate, policy circles, scientific forums, and business roundtables.

In this new scenario, students are emerging as important stakeholders. Many concerned students are rejecting the prevailing economic system. They are challenging business-as-usual because they believe businesses are doing what they believe businesses should not be doing. Indeed, student criticism and opposition to the jobs and to the courses that prepare them for those jobs were expressed in the occupy movements that had spread to various campuses worldwide in the wake of the "Occupy Wall Street" protests. The commitment of the students to various causes—environmental, minority rights and discrimination, colonialism, to name a few—is now as intense as it was in the 1960s and 1970s. These positions often relate to a particular struggle, but they are expressed through the same radical idea that the world needs to be fundamentally changed and that "another world" is possible.

Students in higher education are the most vocal in expressing these critical or radical standpoints. Engineering and business schools may appear to be less dissenting than arts and humanities or law faculties, though this difference seems to be diminishing insofar as some would be engineers and businesspeople refuse to be complicit in a system that seems unacceptable to them (see the now viral video of the AgroParisTech students, for example). The contemporary challenge of ecological transition does call not only for a "fight for values" but also for a transformation of the industrial and economic system. However, it would be an illusion to believe that the ecological transition does not involve a profound change in the values on which the economic system is based. Some students are well aware of this.

For example, the "Wakeup call on the Environment" Manifesto launched in 2018 by students from French business and engineering schools, followed by Swedish, British, German, and Spanish schools, is a call to higher education institutions to take the ecological crisis seriously and to bring about the changes that this awareness demands. Within business schools, there has been an increase in the number of student associations campaigning for behaviours that are more respectful of the planet through ecogestures or for a more radical transformation of our consumerist society and a fossil-fuel-dependent economy through awareness-raising initiatives. If business schools are changing, it is because students are changing. Even the most traditional outlets for business school students—the financial industry, consultancy firms, auditing firms, large multinational groups—are now under increasing pressure from the new regulations that some countries are adopting, the vigilant scrutiny of NGOs, the media, and even the courts. This "ecological turn" also concerns the research carried out in business schools. The criteria used by the *Financial Times* to rank schools now take into account professors' contributions to the debate on the ecological transition.

Although business schools have been put under pressure, it must be said that they have not remained passive in the face of the challenge of ecological transition taken up by protest movements and pioneering academics. Within only a few years, a large number of business schools have made the ecological transition a theme to be included, in varying proportions, in their curricula and have even set up degree and short training programmes dedicated to sustainability. Some schools have chosen to make the ecological transition the main topic of some courses, while others have modified teaching in the core courses—marketing, finance, management, accounting, law, supply-chain, to name a few—to take account of the requirements of sustainable development and the ecological transition. In addition to courses, business schools have also developed research activities, such as seminars, and awareness-raising activities, such as panel discussions, focusing on the ecological transition.

Business schools—a historical perspective

In the early 17th century, armed with investors' money and the blessing of the ruling monarch, several East India Companies sprang up in Europe that set out to exploit colonies in the east. Adventurous young men boarded ships and set sail for faraway lands in search of fortune. Raw materials extracted from the colonies were converted into manufactured goods in British factories to be sold in Britain, Europe, the United States, and back in the colonies. The investors' accumulated capital, a surge of entrepreneurial spirit, technological advances, and consumerism laid the foundations of industrial capitalism. Since the advent of the first industrial revolution in Britain, and later in Europe and the United States, a series of technological revolutions has brought about a sweeping change in economic and social organization all over the world. Business, for the newly industrializing countries, became a force for good. Human lives were no more "solitary, poor, nasty, brutish, and short". The change was made possible not by Hobbes's all-powerful Leviathan who could dictate humans but by free—although often unfair—trade and enterprise.

A key ingredient in this process was the manager. Although not called a business school, Haileybury College, setup near London in 1806 but disbanded in 1858, trained its graduates to oversee commercial transactions of the British East India Company in India. Lord Curzon, erstwhile Viceroy of India, who was appointed the Chancellor of Oxford in 1907, had proposed a two-year business studies course at Oxford. However, business education was not considered an academic discipline at that time. Similar attempts to set up business training programmes at Cambridge—here by Alfred Marshall—had failed. In France, however, several *Grandes Ecoles* had emerged outside the public university system, often in collaboration with chambers of commerce and industry. These elite academic institutes were founded to train leaders for a career in business. Meanwhile, in the United States, business schools were housed within universities and had grown in numbers. By 1915, more than 25 business schools were founded in the United States. The following year, the American Association of Collegiate Schools of Business (AACSB) was founded to transform business schools into professional schools. Formal business education programmes launched in the United States were studied closely by university administrators elsewhere and the post-war period saw the advent of business schools worldwide.

The history of business schools is centred on full-time salaried managers, an occupational category that has gained significant recognition since the late 19th century. In large, limited liability corporations, managers—especially the top executives—have emerged as the more powerful agents compared with other competing groups such as shareholders or shop-floor workers. Business schools have taught generations of students who went on to make big decisions for businesses all over the world. Yet, instead of managing organizations, business school students have increasingly tended to opt for flamboyant careers in finance or consulting. Critics have lamented that business school students are more focused on making money for themselves and are often driven by short-term goals and incentives that encourage reckless decisions with little or no downside risk.

Business schools on the edge of transition

The business school has changed even more in the last two decades. Nowadays business school graduates not only aspire for jobs in finance and consulting. Technology has changed the trajectory of careers as evidenced by the flood of neologisms such as foodtech, fintech, edtech, medtech, or proptech. Courses on data analytics, machine learning, blockchain, and artificial intelligence are on demand. The rapidly changing business environment also means more emphasis on lifelong learning as managers need to constantly update their skillsets. Moreover, the MBA is not the only degree programme offered by business schools. A large range of programmes is on offer, and students can access them online, joining from home, workplace, or another campus on another continent. Propelled by the rankings criteria since the late 1980s and the opening up of new markets in Asia and Africa, business schools nowadays have numerous partner institutions, offer many dual-degree and exchange programmes, and have offices in more than one continent. On a positive note, business schools have become more gender equal over the years—a clear sign of progress.

The business school is an important stakeholder in the globalized world. Today, if there are two trends that are global, they are concerns about sustainability and aspirations about digital technologies. They have usually taken their own distinct paths, but a common element is carbon-intensive technological progress. Digital technologies are changing how billions of people work, live, connect, and consume. On the other hand, the crisis of climate change and resource depletion is affecting all humans. While high growth in the newly industrializing economies is taking millions of people out of poverty, unbridled industrialization for many years has been linked to other crises such as resource depletion and global warming. "Business as usual" is increasingly becoming difficult to conduct because of numerous environmental and regulatory challenges. The building blocks of the public corporation—legal personality, limited liability, and separation of ownership and control—have made them externalizing machines despite a highly developed regulatory system. In this scenario, what should responsible business leaders do to set new standards of managing business? How should they manage the short term and the long term? Is environmental degradation an inevitable consequence of the pursuit of profit? In sum, the ecological crisis makes us rethink the purpose of business and the business school.

One obvious solution is to exercise restraint in the pursuit of economic growth and regulating human activity. This necessitates creating awareness about the finite resources that we have on earth and making judicious use of those resources. An alternative perspective is the relentless pursuit of technological innovation and leaving competition to take care of the outcomes. It is unclear, however, that faith in technological innovations and startups will address issues such as climate change and biodiversity loss. In this "war of all against all", as Hobbes might have described the climate change crisis, we do not have a Leviathan who can impose restraint on all humans. Perhaps the answer is somewhere in the middle. Managers need to judiciously pursue both innovation and restraint. Business schools are aware of the challenges ahead. Barriers to climate change research include lack of funds, expertise, awareness, cross-programme policy, and the complex and interdisciplinary nature of the research. Yet, although knowledge in business schools privilege detached analysis over involved action, there is conformist pressure from stakeholders to embed sustainable development, responsible management, critical thinking, and an understanding of business–society interaction in the regular curriculum. A new management playbook in the light of social and environmental challenges needs to be written.

The book

This book is our attempt to bring together the wide gamut of research interests of our colleagues on the common theme of ecological transition, providing insights for both business and higher education. It includes chapters from 16 professors affiliated with six different departments at ESSEC: Management; Accounting and Management Control; Economics; Information Systems; Decision Sciences and Statistics; Marketing; and Public and Private Policy.

Part I of this book focuses on the big picture required for a radical change in how both corporates and citizens perceive the necessity for ecological transition. The chapter by Vincenzo Esposito Vinzi and co-authors dives into the trust factors that determine public support for pro-environmental initiatives in developed and developing countries, and how governments and businesses can adapt their strategies to encourage these. In what might be termed "from sinners to saints", Stefan Gröschl illustrates how companies, mindset, and governance can form the cornerstone to sustainability transition. And finally, through the lens of paradigm shift, Fabrice Cavarretta explores how collective action can be shaped to move towards a new, shared paradigm on ecological transition that can occur despite the differences of the various stakeholders involved.

Part II of the book brings perspective on sustainability and the need for transparency and accountability. Adrian Zicari tackles the limitations of conventional financial accounting, providing ways in which to move from a purely financial result-based approach to models—both international and local-specific—to measuring corporate impact on social and environmental dimensions. Sustainability necessarily includes not only humans but all sentient beings impacted by humankind's industrial activities. Should businesses account for animal welfare? In an interview with Tom Gamble, Mark Christensen and Geoffrey Lamberton share their views on the topic of animal welfare in the context of live sheep export from Australia and propose an accounting framework that measures animal welfare performance indicators. Lastly, Geneviève Helleringer discusses the issue of greenwashing in product marketing and put the lens on several key EU efforts to ensure transparent and responsible reporting and conduct.

Part III of this book on ecological transition traces the path from product and profit to responsible innovation. Xavier Pavie explores the concept and origins of responsible innovation, how CSR can provide a catalyst for it to spread through corporate culture, and the necessary concerns that business must incorporate in their product innovation to ensure the positive, sustainable outcomes for people, planet, and profit. Furthermore, Emmanuelle Le Nagard sheds light on the complex interplay between perceived obsolescence and consumer decision-making, providing valuable insights for marketers and policymakers.

In Part IV of the book, we put the spotlight on three examples of sustainability engagement that attempt to achieve a shift towards sustainability and the ecological transition. The first of these, written by Laurence de Carlo, takes up the role of education itself, with a focus on a ground-breaking initiative at ESSEC Business School that takes a pragmatic approach to designing a course on energy transition. The second example by Marie-Léandre Gomez highlights the role of CSR and sustainability in the state health system with a focus on hospitals—one of largest emitters of CO_2 and waste—and how to tackle the conflictual boundaries within these organizations to bring about collective and mutually agreed sustainability initiatives. Lastly, Viviane de Beaufort demonstrates the rise and positive impact of shareholder activism that challenges boards and CEOs to shape their role in the sustainability transformation of their firms.

The ecological transition is not only the hobbyhorse or responsibility of developed economies. In Part V of this book, we take into account two major players—and some might say models—in action towards renewable energies: For Asia, this is China, and for Africa, this is Morocco. As the world's largest emitter of greenhouse gases, China is often viewed as a prime sinner, although in reality, it is also the world's biggest producer of renewable energy and the world leader in sustainability-related patents. Cédomir Nestorovic explores several mega-projects undertaken by China and the sustainability and geopolitical implications of these projects both regionally and globally. Morocco is often cited as a model in its energy-transition policies for ecological transition in Africa. In this chapter, Hugues Bouthinon-Dumas and Hamid Bouchikhi shine light on the driving forces behind its strategy to develop green energy, its implementation, the outcomes and ways forward to create a new dynamic in its bid to go green as a locomotive for Africa and beyond.

The book is meant to provide insights to a wide audience. It is for students wishing to grasp the consequences of a transition towards sustainability from a broad perspective. It is for companies, financial institutions, and professionals who wish to gain perspectives on upcoming developments beyond current regulatory requirements, as well as insights on academic research on the grand challenges of sustainability and the transitions related to it. Finally, it will be of interest for instructors seeking insight and learning content, in addition to higher education institutions that are in the process of adjusting their teaching and research to the paradigm shift due to the transition towards sustainability. Each chapter is accompanied by key takeaways and food for thought. We hope you find it useful.

Hugues Bouthinon-Dumas
Arijit Chatterjee
Bernard Leca

Acknowledgements

With kind acknowledgements to Tom Gamble of ESSEC Business School and the Council on Business & Society for copyediting.

Part I

From sinners to saints? How companies, mindsets, and paradigms can contribute to sustainability transition?

1 Shaping citizens' attitudes to engage in climate action in the global south and global north

Vincenzo Esposito Vinzi, Estefania Santacreu-Vasut, Radu Vranceanu and Cristina Davino

Climate crisis: a shared concern from global south to global north

The last 20 or 30 years have seen that the negative impacts of climate change become a major issue of concern for both policymakers and citizens and the focus of much academic research. This has spurred private and public organisations—including governments—to multiply policies and initiatives in support of the environment, increase awareness of the issues at hand, and promote responsible behaviours. However, to a large degree, the success of these policies and initiatives remain dependent on public support.

Past studies—the first tackling the issue of environmental preferences being carried out in the 1970s—focused on the level of a country's wealth or affluence as triggers for supporting environmental matters. The theory is that once a level of wealth obtained in developed economies, citizens turn to "post-materialistic values" such as intellectual, spiritual and aesthetic goals and causes. These include care for the planet and the safeguarding of future generations and find their expression through a global concern for the environment.

Today, however, increasing awareness and pressure from citizens to deal with environmental-related problems have also occurred in developing countries. Typically, these countries face extreme environmental challenges that include waste management, water and air pollution, large-scale drought and, inversely, flooding due to radical fluctuations in climate behaviour. Indeed, research in recent years has shown a convergence of awareness in environmental issues globally and equally between developed and developing countries.

Much of that research has been based on country-specific observations that are then compared with others. These studies have used both objective—for example, environmental quality, education and income—and subjective—awareness of environmental issues and political orientation—factors. Some have focused on environmental activism, with results linked to GDP per capita and how much interviewees are willing to pay for climate action in the guise of environment-related taxes and legislation, for example.

However, the urgency and scale of the climate crisis, in addition to international and national pressures to drastically reduce emissions of greenhouse

DOI: 10.4324/9781003522355-2

gas by the mid of the century, makes the understanding of why people believe, support and take action in climate initiatives extremely important. Does the level of engagement differ from developed to developing countries, from rich to emerging economies? And what makes the basis of action—trust—happen?

What influences individual support for climate action?

In light of the above, our research chose to focus on subjective factors affecting people's pro-environmental behaviour, their concern for the environment and the associated beliefs in this. These amount to the level of people's awareness of environmental challenges, their trust in not-for-profit organisations, trust in for-profit organisations, trust in people and finally trust in technology.

An important determining factor for citizen support for environmental action is awareness. Indeed, despite doubt and mistrust in the early 1980s, there is now general—and strong—belief that climate change is actually happening and has anthropogenic causes. This has occurred through increasing scientific evidence, as well as hands-on experience of the acceleration in climate change. Developing countries in particular allow a "real-time" observation of the impact of economic development on such things as water and air pollution that have a negative impact on public health. But there still remain people—sometimes at the highest level of governance—who dismiss the idea that climate change is linked to human economic activity.

At a national level, collective perceptions of environmental changes can be shaped or hindered by a country's economic history, the economic and environmental knowledge of the population and its politics related to its economic interests. An example here would be the relationship of Japanese citizens to nuclear power and the impression the Fukushima disaster of 2011 has instilled in them.

Social capital—the set of shared values and resources that enables people to work together for a common cause—may also have an influence on people's attitudes to environmental policies. This is because environmental issues call upon more than mere market-based decisions and dig deep into factors such as trust, citizenship and collective well-being. Indeed, research has demonstrated that societies in which people have a high level of trust in others are more likely to commit to global cooperation and the fight to reduce GHG emissions. However, because climate action necessarily involves governments and business, people's trust in these—as well as technology—may either help or create obstacles to the implementation of policy. Moreover, climate action often involves costs to the population in the form, for example, of carbon taxes, the adoption of electric vehicles which remain costly for many segments of the population, or penalties on the purchase of certain goods.

In democracies, the tendency might be for governments to hold off policy for fear of losing votes. And it is here that the key factors of trust and subsequent public support in the government might gain the adoption of unpopular, but necessary, measures. Nevertheless, this could be questioned, especially regarding developing countries, where government corruption may lead to low confidence in the population. After all, could a government effectively deal with environmental problems when it cannot find local solutions for infrastructure and healthcare?

It is in this light that the role of non-profit organisations becomes important. In many instances, NGOs, media outlets and associations can contribute to environmental protection by providing information, educating, giving information on eco-friendly technologies and goods, and ways to consume in a greener, more planet-friendly way.

A third influencer comes in the form of trust in science and technology and their ability to solve the world's big problems. Indeed, in the environmental field, technological progress has been at the forefront of continuous innovations leading to reductions in the cost to produce renewable energies, the enhancement and performance of batteries for electric vehicles, or design features aimed at minimising fuel consumption in both the car- and aircraft-manufacturing sectors to name but a few. Greentech has also benefited from scientific advances which have helped to reduce pollution and consumption of energy per unit of production.

However, not all is rosy regarding green. Despite technological progress, tech's capacity to alleviate and diminish damage to the environment has been slow, as world economies continue to grow, population levels rise and greater levels of consumption per capita are reached. Decoupling—growth of GDP rising while CO_2 emissions fall—is happening in many countries, but not at a sufficient pace to achieve the UN climate targets. Investment in green R&D also conceals a drawback—R&D being negatively correlated with the fluctuations in fossil energy prices. Indeed, trust and the resulting enthusiasm for tech solutions to fight against climate change are something of a double-edged sword. On the one hand, strong enthusiasm for it can negatively affect pro-environmental behaviour—people tending to rely on possible future innovations to remove environmental risks rather than engage in changing their behaviour and acting responsibly in their consumer and consumption decisions. Inversely, trust in tech can encourage pro-environmental behaviour in the sense that people take scientific evidence on the causes and results of climate change that much more seriously. All in all, attitudes to science and technology play an important part in decisions—both individual and governmental—on whether to take climate action to protect and improve the environment.

A final influencer could be the trust individuals place in the private sector and in private companies to act responsibly towards the environment. CSR—corporate social responsibility—having long-since incorporated the sustainable development dimension within its portfolio of action has been at the forefront of many initiatives in the field, including the carbon disclosure project launched in 2000 for companies, investors, cities and regions to manage their environmental impact, or the Science Based Targets initiative that helps companies implement emissions reduction policies. But here again, the flip side to the coin is that people's trust in such corporate engagement can lead to a *disengagement* on their part—leaving the job for others to undertake and reducing their support for environmental action.

In addition, the level of trust in private companies can differ from country to country. This depends on country-specific regulations but also on the type of sector in which a company finds itself. For while every firm consumes energy, some, such as water, gas or energy distributors, textile or fossil fuel and cement manufacturers, count among the highest emitters of GHG. On the other hand, government regulations in certain countries can be stricter than others in sanctioning the big gas-belchers through carbon taxes or Emission Trading Rights. Lastly, in developed economies, people's trust in firms can be shaped by country-specific visions of what CSR is—in the United States, for example, characterised by voluntary participation in social and environmental practices, and in Europe largely guided by EU or country-specific law and regulations.

Under the research lens

Taking the aforementioned influencers—awareness of environmental stakes and challenges, trust in not-for-profit and for-profit organisations, trust in people and finally trust in technology—we sought to explore which influencing factors have the most effect in both developed and developing countries in committing to pro-environmental action.

To do so, we analysed data reported by the 2008 and 2014 waves of the World Values Survey, including 35,000 individuals from 42 countries; in the aggregate, we also specifically explored four key economies among the world's largest polluters—China, India, the United States and Germany. Results were published in *Social Indicators Research* (Davino et al., 2019).

Awareness of environmental issues and stakes

Overall, and as could be expected, personal awareness—the initial stage in any learning process that leads to a change in skill or behaviour—has a positive effect on individuals' commitment to action. However, this influence is weaker in developing countries—unsurprising given the double challenge of findings solutions to protect the planet while at the same time under pressure to develop high economic growth to catch up with developed countries. The awareness of citizens of developing countries tended to focus on poor air quality rather than water quality, poor sewage and waste management.

Focusing on the big four polluters, the findings pointed towards environmental awareness in the United States and Germany being a chief driver of people's decisions to take action. This importance turned out to be lower in China and hardly significant in India.

Trust in not-for-profit and for-profit organisations

Trust in non-profits too was found to have a positive impact on individual action, particularly NGOs. Here, people in developed countries would be readier to focus their support for environmental action through paying higher taxes or donating to NGOs active in environmental protection or climate action initiatives, compared to people in emerging economies.

The study revealed the flip side of the coin—that people trusting for-profit companies expressed a lower level of support for paying higher taxes or sacrificing income to finance environmental policies. As mentioned previously, this might reflect the fact that people shift some or all of their responsibility in taking climate action to the companies in which they entrust to undertake action and initiative. This reflected the trend in both Germany and the United States and also matches the pattern seen for developed countries in general—the mindset being that if companies can protect the environment, human action is less necessary.

Moreover, companies in developed countries have been communicating on their green initiatives for over 20 years as part of their CSR policy, again hinting to the effect that citizens might step back from individual action while letting the corporates get on with the task. A difference lies in India, where trust in private companies does indeed have a positive, triggering effect on individuals' desire to commit to act for the environment.

Science and technology

Our findings also revealed that trust in science and technology has a positive effect on individual action, or that they help shape positive attitudes towards environmental policy by making it easier to understand the reasons behind climate change and the results that follow. Overall, attitudes are similar between developed and developing countries, but interestingly enough, there are differences in the magnitude of the effects. While people in developing countries put stronger importance on the future benefits of science and technology, inversely those in developed countries put lesser importance on these determinants.

At odds with the average tendency observed in the full sample is the example of Germany. Here, trust in tech has a negative effect on support towards the environment, with people softening their vigilance of environmental issues. This can be attributed to the fact that, traditionally, Germany has maintained a high level of manufacturing capability in terms of share of GDP, and that science and technology have long been the upholders of innovations in ever-efficient—and presumably leaner, cleaner—industry.

Towards greater environmental action

Our findings point towards several areas where governments, non-profits and companies can tweak their initiatives in order to encourage greater action on an individual level from their citizens and consumers. It cannot be left to international rules alone, for despite general global consensus that humankind has to take strong and, to a large extent, voluntary action in favour of the environment, progress is slow. It also, at times, takes a step backwards—as witnessed by the US withdrawal from the Paris Agreement in 2017 (then joined again in 2021 under the new Democrat Administration). People and their trust are therefore important factors to trigger transition from the bottom up while governments and international bodies attempt a simultaneous top-down approach.

Overall, personal awareness is a key element, stronger in the developed world than the developing, and it begs the suggestion that there is room for improvement in communication initiatives in favour of the environment in these countries.

Trust in science and technology is generally strong determinant of pro-climate action in every country featured in the survey—again with some minor variations, hinting towards governments and corporations consolidating their investment in these fields. True, trust in companies seems to have an inverse effect in developed economies. Here, communicating too much on their positive actions and results in sustainability unintentionally seems to make people less inclined to want to support taxes and policies that attempt to contribute to climate action. Once again, an appropriate amount of communication and a good dose of modesty might do the trick in shifting citizen support.

As an upshot of all these, beliefs, emotions and attitudes play an important role in shaping individual action in favour of environmentally friendly policies. Governments would be wise to take these factors into account when designing new and responsible polices. Investment in improving how government institutions and NGOs work and perform might also have much positive impact in fostering support for green policies, as well as developing public–private partnerships in the fight against climate change. All in all, awareness and trust are present—in both rich and developing economies. It might do for that awareness and trust to be nudged and encouraged across the globe, and across all stakeholders, to energise the undeniable need to act and effectively address the climate crisis.

Key takeaways:

- Climate change and climate crisis have become major issues in the past two decades. Private and public organisations—including governments—have multiplied policies and initiatives in support of the environment.
- To a large degree, the success of these policies and initiatives remains dependent on public support. It is therefore crucial to understand what can foster citizens' trust in order for them to support and commit to climate action.

- Awareness, countries' economic and cultural maps, social capital, trust in NGOs and private companies, and trust in science and technology all shape people's engagement (or not) with pro-environment action.

This research has revealed the following:

- Awareness has a positive effect on individuals' commitment to action. However, this influence is weaker in developing countries which deal simultaneously with environmental challenges and pressure to develop their economies.
- Trust in non-profits was found to have a positive impact on individual action, particularly NGOs. People in developed countries would be readier to focus their support for environmental action through paying higher taxes or donating to NGOs active in environmental protection or climate action initiatives.
- People trusting for-profit companies express a lower level of support for paying higher taxes or sacrificing income to finance environmental policies, reflecting a "responsibility shift" to corporates.
- Trust in science and technology has a positive effect on individual action, helping shape positive attitudes towards environmental policy by making it easier to understand the reasons behind climate change.
- While people in developing countries put stronger importance on the future benefits of science and technology, those in developed countries put lesser importance on these determinants—most probably due to the fact that science and technology have already provided multiple solutions and results in these countries.
- Future recommendations include improvement in communication initiatives to boost awareness, less communication and "marketing" of corporate CSR and sustainability initiatives to reduce citizens' "responsibility shift", the taking into account of beliefs, emotions and attitudes when designing policies, improving government and NGO functioning and developing public–private partnerships.

Food for thought:

- Think of your country. How does it rate in terms of awareness of climate change and the extent of initiatives to combat climate crisis? What could be done better?
- What about you personally? What actions do you take? What spurred you to take action? And who do you trust most—your government, non-profits and NGOs, or companies to effectively tackle climate-related issues?
- To what extent do you think it is the moral duty for developed countries to contribute most to tackling climate crisis? Why? How?
- To what extent should citizens pay the price for climate change by reducing their consumption, changing their behaviours, paying climate taxes?

Or should we entrust science and technological innovation to find the solutions while maintaining our way of life?

Related research (including references in the above text):

Davino, C., Esposito Vinzi, V., Santacreu-Vasut, E., & Vranceanu, R. (2019). An attitude model of environmental action: Evidence from developing and developed countries. *Social Indicators Research*, *143*(2), 811–838. https://doi.org/10.1007/s11205-018-1983-3

2 Responsible leadership and sustainable business practices

Stefan Gröschl

Why do businesses vary in their engagement toward the sustainable use of the environment and its common-pool resources? What motivates company leaders to develop business models that address economic and environmental demands simultaneously? And finally, what is the role of business schools in preparing students for addressing today's complex global socio-economic and environmental challenges in a sustainable and responsible way?

I base the discussion of these three questions on my work with Tobias Hahn and Patricia Gabaldon on responsible leadership and corporate sustainability. Moreover, in our studies, we addressed socio-economic and environmental aspects from an organizational perspective, a micro-foundations perspective, and a business school perspective.

The growth of the notion of responsible leadership

The concept of responsible leadership emerged in the early 2000s, spurred by Maak and Pless (2006) and Waldman and Galvin's work (2008), and drawing on Ed Freeman's seminal work on stakeholder theory (1984).

Indeed, proponents of responsible leadership argue that companies and their leaders 'are expected to be accountable not only to shareholders for financial performance, but to stakeholders for their wider economic, environmental and societal impacts' (Wade, 2006, p. 227). Another key figure is entrepreneur John Elkington, who, in his 1997 book *Cannibals with Forks: The Triple Bottom Line of the 21st Century Business*, contended that businesses should base their operations on positively impacting not only profit (shareholders) and people (employees and stakeholders) but also the planet in a conscious bid to tackle the negative environmental effects brought about by industrialization and consumerism. These formed the now famous three Ps of the triple bottom line: People, Planet, and Profit.

In effect amounting to corporate sustainability, the concept gained global attention in 2015, when the United Nations adopted 17 sustainable development goals (SDGs) to advance peace, prosperity, and positive impact for people and the planet.

DOI: 10.4324/9781003522355-3

It is important here to mention the concept of common-pool resources—natural or public assets that have a finite supply—and are part of environmental ecosystems that include groundwater basins, lakes, fisheries, and forests. Characterized by their finite nature, high subtractability, and low excludability, they are subject to what is termed the *tragedy of the commons*, where individuals (or businesses) acting for their own benefit, in effect, over-consume the resource, thereby depleting it for all.

From free riders to altruistic firms

In my 2014 study with Patricia Gabaldon (Gabaldon and Gröschl, 2014), we argued that firms and their business activities that contribute to the maintaining of common-pool resources were at an embryonic stage. At the time of the study, we identified economic constraints and bottom-line interests, short-term perspectives, and shareholder expectations as the 'usual suspects' that superseded a sense of moral duty among numerous private businesses to engage in the sustenance of common-pool resources. Considering the many calls for an urgent rethinking of how to do business due to growing environmental damage and excess use of common-pool resources, we wondered what the motives were that drive or hinder businesses' contributions to common-pool resources.

As such, we categorized companies according to their contributions to common-pool resources. The companies' positioning depended on the pro/reactiveness of their actions and behaviors toward the use of common-pool resources, and the nature of the underlying reasons for their actions—for example, self-interest and short-term oriented versus sustainability and long-term oriented.

Identifying four categories of a company, we termed these *free riders*, *followers*, *believers*, and *altruists*. Let's have a look at them. Free riding companies act solely in their own self-interest and are driven by short-term profit maximization. Followers are 'skeptical' companies whose actions contributing to common-pool resources are driven both by company self-interest and by reactions to external forces such as compliance with legislation. Believing companies, on the other hand, need some encouragement from a forerunner, or company that they can follow and trust to engage in sustainable business activities. And, finally, altruistic firms act sustainably and believe intrinsically in the benefits and positive consequences of their actions for common-pool resources.

We connected our categories of firms and their sustainability engagement with the notion of social trapping—situations where people or companies choose to opt for short-term benefits regardless of the unpleasant or lethal consequences at a later stage and which cannot be easily changed. From this matching, we were able to provide companies and other stakeholders with a differentiating perspective that allows for propositions that address the complex nature of motivational structures and common-pool resources.

As such, distinguishing between companies' motives helps business leaders, institutions, and policymakers to develop more tailored solutions that contribute to common-pool resources in a sustainable way. Moreover, these solutions differ from actions that solely serve organizational self-interests and combine both internal and external incentives that help firms to change organizational motives and interests toward common-pool resources. Two example of this are employee well-being and greater employee engagement. Notably, in terms of external catalysts for the transition toward sustainable operations, we emphasized collective arrangements and partnerships between firms based on mutual trust and collaboration and that adapt to local contexts and complexities.

From business as usual to sustainability pioneers

An interesting case of a company transitioning toward a sustainable business model, and the focus of research carried out with Patricia Gabaldon and Tobias Hahn, is that of Jochen Zeitz, Puma's CEO from 1993 to 2011 (Gröschl et al., 2019). We looked at the motives behind Zeitz that made him change his approach from doing business as usual to doing business in a sustainable and responsible way.

More specifically, we wanted to grasp a better understanding of how Zeitz's cognitive complexity—his thoughts and perceptions—influenced his opinion and initiatives on sustainability over time. Indeed, while it is generally agreed that managerial acquisition of knowledge and understanding plays an important role in determining corporate responses to sustainability, very little research focused on the role of leaders' cognitive complexity for explaining this.

Analyzing multiple sources, including press articles, corporate news, videos, company reports, and expert interviews, to better understand the increasing cognitive complexity of Jochen Zeitz as Puma CEO during the period from 1993 to 2011, we found that Zeitz developed increasingly complex cognitive patterns over time that went hand in hand with his understanding of, and proactive strategic responses to, sustainability. This went beyond narrow business imperatives—as illustrated by Puma's environmental profit and loss account (EPL). The EPL effectively quantifies environmental externalities by placing a monetary value on environmental impacts along the entire value chain of a business. The result is a profit and loss statement that includes the full costs of a company's environmental impact in financial terms, making a company's environmental externalities transparent and comparable. Moreover, Puma's EPL was celebrated as the first comprehensive EPL to be applied by a company.

The EPL was one of many key events and experiences in the biography of Zeitz that we juxtaposed with the evolution of his views and initiatives on sustainability. And by doing so, we were able to identify how his perceptions, understanding, and stance toward sustainability co-evolved. Ultimately, his managerial cognition was shaped by six different cognitive lenses that emerged and integrated over time, influencing his understanding of

- the interrelationship of profitability and a sustainable approach to conducting business;
- different national and organizational cultures characterized by different perspectives and views about doing business;
- the interdependencies between communities, environments, and businesses operating within an ecosystem at a micro level;
- challenging existing norms and traditions;
- fundamental questions and challenges of life, and the individual and collective responsibilities to address these challenges;
- changing demands of (potential) consumers and other stakeholders for greater environmental consciousness and sustainable business actions.

Zeitz's cognitive development coincided with his approach toward sustainability changing from a rather narrow, business-only focus, toward a holistic one that resulted in proactive sustainability initiatives such as the EPL.

Indeed, proactive strategic responses to sustainability may well require leaders to develop more complex cognitive patterns over time. In other words, leaders need to develop and grow their horizon beyond narrow commercial concerns, especially in global businesses that face sensitive social and environmental issues.

We also found evidence that supports the argument that managers with more complex cognitive frames are more likely to 'consider responses that break with established routines and business practices in order to achieve environmental and social benefits at the societal level' (Hahn et al., 2014, p. 478).

Our findings subsequently raised several questions worth asking for any future research project—whether, for example, the successful development and implementation of innovative sustainability initiatives necessarily needs to start from a business-oriented perspective. Or whether business success in the first place is a precondition for the co-evolution of cognitive complexity and proactive sustainability—and within the same context. And, even whether a similar co-evolution between cognitive complexity and proactive sustainability might be expected.

Preparing for sustainability: from disciplinary to transdisciplinary thinking in business school education

Another study published together with Patricia Gabaldon in 2016 (Gröschl & Gabaldon, 2016), we explored business schools and their role of preparing future decision-makers to lead businesses in a sustainable and responsible way. Our interest in this topic was sparked by our previous studies on the different organizational responses and attitudes toward sustainability as outlined earlier.

We proposed French philosopher and sociologist Edgar Morin's notion of transdisciplinarity as a complementary educational perspective for preparing business school students in addressing the complex socio-economic and environmental challenges that societies across the globe have been facing for some time; and by doing so, developing organizational changes that transform firms from free riders to altruists (Morin, 2008).

Morin described transdisciplinarity as a concept that extends beyond multidisciplinary or interdisciplinary approaches that are limited in coordination, interaction, and cooperation (Morin, 2008).

Morin's transdisciplinary approach is problem focused and inquiry driven, instead of being dictated or limited by disciplinary boundaries. Moreover, Morin's transdisciplinarity holds a systemic vision that challenges the continuous separation of humanism and science, and the fragmentation of their disciplines.

It can be contended that the separation of academic disciplines and focus on analytical thinking has created a reductionist approach to problem solving that causes students to reduce things to black-and-white choices or realities. It goes without saying that this tends to reinforce simplistic thinking, preventing students from being able to address complex phenomena such as sustainability by making sense of their connection to the whole and vice versa.

Returning to Edgar Morin, a transdisciplinary perspective requires a form of thinking based on distinction, conjunction, and implication rather than disjunction and reduction. In this way, Morin transforms linear causal thinking into an approach where differing perspectives are interrelated and interconnected, allowing for a better understanding of the uncertainties and complexities that come with sustainability (Morin, 2008).

Such a perspective supports students in their exploration and unification of concepts that are simultaneously complementary and contradictory in nature. In particular, within the sustainability context, such conceptual challenges are evident when firms are under pressure to integrate often-competing economic, environmental, and social aspects at the same time. When facing such complex and competing challenges, Morin's transdisciplinarity does not focus on 'either-or' solutions—it proposes to re-combine, re-engage, and re-connect scientific knowledge with philosophical reflections and reflexive knowledge (Morin, 2008).

Taking the proposition of transdisciplinarity as a complementary educational perspective into account, we addressed the criticism of business schools and of the relevance of their curricula and teaching methods in preparing business leaders and decision-makers to respond in a sustainable way to the complex challenges that they face. For a transdisciplinary teaching approach to work, professors from different disciplines need to be encouraged to collaboratively teach courses and programs that are inquiry driven rather than discipline driven. Moreover, they need to focus on broader questions, fundamental questions, and complex challenges that business leaders currently face when it comes to sustainable business models and strategies.

Given that corporate sustainability is characterized by frequently competing demands, professors would be wise to foster systemic perspectives on the subject of inquiry—and by doing so, help students learn to connect seemingly contradictory and opposing demands. Transdisciplinary-oriented courses should also aim to develop cyclic thinking—particularly in regard to exploring and evaluating the cause-and-effect relationships that shape sustainability solutions, and through which students' actions and decisions are governed. Various perspectives and types of knowledge presented through these courses can help students examine their actions from within and across systems, and to consider the implications of their decisions and actions for different stakeholders inside and outside of organizations.

One initiative at ESSEC Business School that deserves emphasis is the 'ESSEC iMagination Week' which provides a concrete example of teaching beyond disciplines. Here, during one full week, students are confronted with abstract themes such as transformation, or broad topics such as work and life. In both plenary sessions and small groups, students meet and work with experts with very diverse backgrounds and experiences ranging from life sciences, future studies, technology, arts, music, cybernetics, maths, meditation, gastronomy, philosophy, astrophysics, ecology, biochemistry, foresight, mobility, and cryptography. By working across disciplinary boundaries, students develop an understanding of the complex issues of the world they are building, strengthen their capacity to think creatively to overcome these issues, and sharpen awareness for tackling the consequences of their decisions.

Another important aspect for consideration in the operationalization of Morin's transdisciplinarity is the development of an intersubjective understanding through critical self-reflection. As Morin himself said, without such self-inquiry, students will consider everything that is distant or foreign as secondary, insignificant or hostile. With such self-inquiry, students develop a moral consciousness that is central to Morin's educational philosophy and transdisciplinary perspective. And with it, students can challenge ideas and theories that are otherwise unconcerned by moral rightness or wrongness and question taken-for-granted differences between facts and values.

In many programs and courses in today's business schools, such critical self-analytical thinking and self-reflective behaviors are already in place. In other words, some of Morin's ideas already exist in one form or another in teaching approaches and business school curricula, and his propositions do not necessarily require radical changes. Ultimately, by developing and extending some of Morin's transdisciplinary propositions, higher education institutions can assist students in becoming responsible business leaders and future decision-makers who engage in a more sustainable future.

A look back at going forward

Shortly after the publication of our research on Morin's transdisciplinarity, Covid-19 hit societies and businesses around the world. The global pandemic highlighted the vulnerability and complexity of different ecosystems, and the interdependencies of stakeholders within and between these systems. At the same time, in 2019, the International Resource Panel warned that if businesses globally do not engage in greater sustainable activities such as decoupling business success from resource use, introducing immediate resource efficiency and circularity measures, building coalitions, and engaging with policymakers, resource use and related impacts would exceed the planetary boundaries and endanger human well-being (International Resource Panel, 2019).

The global pandemic accentuated the salience and relevance of many of the concepts, ideas, practices, and processes mentioned in this text connected to corporate sustainability and responsible leadership. Unfortunately, the war in Ukraine is just one of many events and developments that may prevent us from being overly optimistic that the Covid-19 pandemic has been disruptive enough to amplify firms' efforts to engage in greater sustainable and regenerative actions, and responsible leadership.

Key takeaways:

- Responsible leadership implies that companies and their leaders are expected to be accountable not only to shareholders for financial performance but also to stakeholders for their wider economic, environmental, and societal impact.
- John Elkington framed the three Ps of the triple bottom line—People, Planet, Profit—in effect amounting to corporate sustainability. This was followed by the United Nations 17 sustainable development goals (SDGs).
- Common-pool resources, characterized by their finite nature, high subtractability, and low excludability, are subject to the *tragedy of the commons*, where individuals (or businesses) acting for their own benefit, in effect over-consume the resource, thereby depleting it for all.
- Research identified five categories of company: Free riders acting solely in their own self-interest and are driven by short-term profit maximization. Followers—skeptical firms whose actions contributing to common-pool resources are driven both by company self-interest and by reactions to external forces such as compliance with legislation. Believing companies that require encouragement from a forerunner, or company that they can follow and trust to engage in sustainable business activities. Altruistic firms which act sustainably and believe intrinsically in the benefits and positive consequences of their actions for common-pool resources.
- In the transition toward sustainable operations, companies are recommended to make collective arrangements and partnerships between firms

based on mutual trust and collaboration and that adapt to local contexts and complexities.

- A study of former Puma CEO Jochen Zeitz identified six factors that helped him shape his and Puma's perspective on sustainability: the interrelationship of profitability and a sustainable approach to conducting business; different national and organizational cultures characterized by different perspectives and views about doing business; the interdependencies between communities, environments, and businesses operating within an ecosystem at a micro level; challenging existing norms and traditions; fundamental questions and challenges of life, and the individual and collective responsibilities to address these challenges; and changing demands of (potential) consumers and other stakeholders for greater environmental consciousness and sustainable business actions.
- Leaders need to develop and grow their horizon beyond narrow commercial concerns, especially in global businesses that face sensitive social and environmental issues.
- Preparing future generations of responsible leaders requires business schools to adopt a transdisciplinary approach to educating students.
- This enables students to move away from simplistic black-and-white decision-making to interrelating and interconnecting differing perspectives to better understand the uncertainties and complexities that come with sustainability.

Food for thought:

- Which CEOs and which companies today are representative of responsible leadership and commitment to sustainability?
- What makes them different?
- Think of your studies—either current or past. To what extent did they promote a transdisciplinary approach to learning and forming decisions? How could your education be/have been improved?
- Which factors and experiences have led you to adopt a responsible leadership and sustainability mindset?
- Which three things can you do in the future to foster and improve responsible leadership in your studies, job, or company?

References and related research

Elkington, J. (1997). *Cannibals with forks: The triple bottom line of the 21st century business.* Capstone.

Freeman, R. (1984). *Strategic management: A stakeholder approach.* Pitman Publishers.

Gabaldon, P., & Gröschl, S. (2014). A few good companies: Rethinking firms' responsibilities toward common pool resources. *Journal of Business Ethics*, *132*(3), 579–588.

Gröschl, S., & Gabaldon, P. (2016). Business schools and the development of responsible leaders: A proposition of Edgar Morin's transdisciplinarity. *Journal of Business Ethics*, *153*(1), 185–195.

Gröschl, S., Gabaldon, P., & Hahn, T. (2019). The co-evolution of leaders' cognitive complexity and corporate sustainability: The case of the CEO of Puma. *Journal of Business Ethics*, *155*(3), 741–762.
Hahn, T., Preuss, L., Pinkse, J., & Figge, F. (2014). Cognitive frames in corporate sustainability: Managerial sensemaking with paradoxical and business case frames. *Academy of Management Review*, *39*(4), 463–487.
International Resource Panel. (2019). *Global resources outlook*. www.resourcepanel.org/reports/global-resources-outlook
Maak, T., & Pless, N. (2006). Responsible leadership in a stakeholder society—A relational perspective. *Journal of Business Ethics*, *66*, 99–115. https://doi.org/10.1007/s10551-006-9047-z
Morin, E. (2008). *On complexity*. Hampton Press.
Wade, M. (2006). Developing leaders for sustainable business. In Maak Th., & Pless N.M. (Eds.), *Responsible leadership* (pp. 227–244). Routledge.
Waldman, D., & Galvin, B. (2008). Alternative perspectives of responsible leadership. *Organizational Dynamics*, *37*(4), 327–341.

3 Wishing for a shift

A paradigm perspective on ecological transition

Fabrice Cavarretta

The pressing need of having an impact has gained widespread legitimacy in management studies, coupled with the suggestion that researchers and instructors should contribute to larger societal goals beyond management's modest roots in business administration. As such, management scholars are increasingly called upon to revise the traditional approach that links the values and actions of organizations to their "accomplishing impact" in larger society.

This mandate appears even more crucial when approaching major contemporary issues such as *anthropic climate change*. Intergovernmental Panel on Climate Change (IPCC) reports have repeatedly confirmed the scientific evidence as well as the harmful consequences for human and natural life of an environmentally careless industrial system. As a result, various ways to reduce the negative impact of human activity on climate and the environment have been identified which motivate stakeholders to undertake an *ecological transition*—often formulated as a wish for a *paradigm shift* of our socio-industrial systems.

However, the extent, the boundaries, and the implementation of a transition remain uncertain due to the complexity of such a massive collective upheaval. It entails a deep change in values, attitudes, and behaviours across populations worldwide. On this note, many factors can be said to drive human actions. And at individual and psychological levels, the traditional assumption is that motivation triggers actions. In the case of sustainability, the *need* for an ecological transition may appear as a compelling driving motive. Unfortunately—however burning the issue may be—mere motivational mechanisms do not seem to lead to efficient collective mobilization.

Ecological transition constitutes an utmost collective challenge. As such, it will require what the German sociologist Max Weber labelled *social action*—that is, a sum of collective actions occurring through sensemaking. Social action derives from various factors, starting with *beliefs* but also from *norms*, or even through the subtle effects of *material artifacts—for example*, the products we use, the infrastructure enabling us to travel, or our living spaces.

All those factors constitute, in sort, a constellation which may appear messy and confusing at first. However, their clustering into the concept of *paradigm* makes them manageable in theory and more in practice. Made

DOI: 10.4324/9781003522355-4

originally famous by philosopher Thomas Kuhn in a study of scientific communities in 1962, the concept is often invoked when framing ecological transition as a *paradigm shift*—that is, a holistic and fundamental change in approach and assumptions.

Appearing first in ancient philosophy, Kuhn defined *paradigm* in modern times as "the entire *constellation* of beliefs, values, techniques, *and so on* shared by the members of a given community". Soon enough, to the amazement of Kuhn, the term took a life of its own in the general public. Today, the term is used commonly for any collective practice in any area of life, such as politics, medicine, or sports, to name a few. In search engines, the term "paradigm" is reported at tens of millions of mentions, and "paradigm shift" in millions.

Origins and shifts of paradigms

Paradigm has been invoked with various meanings, first applied to scientists then to practitioners. It sometimes narrows on a cognitive sense, the paradigm amounting to a general idea or a short set of ideas. In other cases, as in Kuhn, it encompasses much larger and open-ended meanings, from cognitive to material, to norms, and to practices, among others.

To describe such reasoning, we can more concisely define the concept of paradigm as *the nexus of social action in a community*.[1] Or, put otherwise, the connection or link between people, things, and events that cause people to act and change. This encompasses all components that determine social action, for example, from conceptual—beliefs, cognitions, theories, values, norms, and emotions—to material—objects, actions, and routines. It also includes all interactions among any of those factors: for example, from values that generate behaviours, from objects that create beliefs, or from beliefs that create values.

Paradigms occur at community level yet instantiated by individuals in that community. The term *instantiation* here means that each individual constitutes a (little) instance of the paradigm that each individual somewhat interprets the paradigm's elements in its own individual way. This may occur across all levels of the social system—from situations to individuals, to groups of individuals, to groups of collectives, and finally to society at large.

Moreover, paradigms emerge out of an evolutionary process of repeated social recombination among people until the collective converges on the shared "bundle" of values, beliefs, and subsequent behaviours that constitute social action. However, if we were to take technology and industry as an example, changes occur not through a series of small steps. Rather, it occurs through distinct phases of dominant design and innovation, as the various stakeholders—companies, their employees, suppliers, and customers—are constrained by the collective tools, mindsets, and ways of doing things. For instance, when the car industry moved towards four-wheeled vehicles and a steering wheel on the left, those parameters became difficult to alter, even if alternative and more efficient designs were to exist. The same goes for social action. It occurs in moments or phases of a shift in perceptions and behaviour that have to contend with and conflict with existing assumptions, beliefs, and ways of doing things.

Paradigm shift and the ecological transition

In this light, the reorganization of the social-economic system required for the ecological transition likely implies a radical change that would occur when sufficient tension has accumulated. One might hope that adjustments would occur naturally and progressively when needed; unfortunately, delays and discontinuities are to be expected.

Moreover, letting the natural course of the transition to occur implies more brutal pain down the road, when the damage to climate and the environment finally has to be reckoned with, potentially with greater magnitude. And since our current growth-based industrial paradigm constitutes a stable truce, where business and society continue largely as usual, making effort towards sustainability but refraining from radical and rapid shift, it tends to fundamentally underestimate the needs for changes.

The gap between the adaptations required to save the environment and their apparent non-urgency does not imply that changes cannot be supported or that we cannot reduce the brutality of unmanaged and too late phase transition. Yet, even under progressive and assisted regime change, we can expect pain to appear in the system until the final reorganization settles in. Drastic challenges such as rapid anthropic climate change require significant investments that will at first appear unjustified; hence, the buildup of a lag that will require a brutal response at later points. This implies perceived pain by all the stakeholders, until adjusted to the new paradigm: those seeing the future pains yearn for it, while those still stuck on the old paradigm resent the apparently useless efforts.

For instance, let's consider the need to alter mobility away from reliance on individual cars fuelled by fossil energy. Obviously, societal and urban development based on individual fossil energy cars has been identified as highly problematic for a long time. Yet experiments at local levels have illustrated the pain of trying to change the system in place. When trying to shift large cities—for example, Paris—from a car-based mobility paradigm and into softer mobilities such as cycling or walking, it first requires moving part of the road system away from cars and towards alternatives—for example, bike lanes. Once done, those adjustments initially appear underused. And for the people whose commute had been based on individual car mobility, the transition puts them under immense pressure when those car-averse measures are implemented—often long before public transport provides fully equivalent alternatives, or long before spatial patterns can be adjusted such as the location of work versus the location of home.

The discontinuous nature of paradigms and their tendency to shift embody the lapse between the need and the adjustment. This implies that pain permeates the whole transition, possibly for all parties involved—from those committed to an old paradigm as well to those yearning for the upcoming one.

Understanding the key components of paradigms to facilitate the ecological transition

Let's now focus on the internal composition of paradigms. We can analyze the notion of paradigm into four broad and overlapping components: *beliefs, objects, values, and performance.* The final dimension, *performance*, captures what actually occurs, which can be consistent—or not—with the intent and beliefs of the various actors involved. These components interact with each other.

For example, someone might value his right to freedom of choice over how to travel and choose to drive a large SUV. He also believes that environmental activists might just be trying to take away this freedom by attempting to ban such vehicles. As a result, he tends to agree with the opposing camp of climate sceptics. But he necessarily comes into contact with and interacts with other drivers in his community who have changed to electric cars. He might, or might not, begin to change his perceptions accordingly once he sees the benefits of electric mobility. In this light, ecological transition may be more about conceiving a sum of steps linking various components of social action than hoping for the overarching powers of one key component such as a central government ban on all combustion-engine vehicles.

A key characteristic that explains the resilience of paradigms is the ability of components to *morph* in various ways. We can illustrate this through the parable of "the three medieval stonecutters". As a passerby asks them about their activity, the first stonecutter responds, "I'm cutting rocks". The second one answer: "I'm earning a living". And the third stonecutter replies: "I'm serving God". Even though the stonecutters accomplish a similar task at the same time, each may represent a distinctively personal instance of the overarching paradigm of their collective—that is, medieval religious society. The parable gives us an example of how people may have diverse ways of making sense of themselves and the world—in this instance by the selective interpretation of a few basic elements: the rocks, the tools, money, and religion. The first stonecutter takes a narrow *practice* interpretation of the activity. The second one takes a *transactional* interpretation. And the last one makes a *value* interpretation.

Notice how specifically the element *church* has a fluctuating role and relationship to other elements. It can appear as the performative objective of a value system—the expected outcome of a job for *rewards*; as a practice system—defining one's identity through the usage of tools to produce such type of architectural output; and as a mediator towards serving a value system—the church serves the belief in God.

In this parable, one may visualize that the medieval society paradigm does not function by having all actors sharing similar values. However, their collective interactions end up serving a moral value (God) and a material object as the church plays a pivotal role in linking social action.

In a paradigmatic approach to ecological transition, one can expect simple objects to play *pivotal* roles, sometimes more importantly than establishing shared values. Returning to the issue of *mobility*, notice that many urban environments around the world have significantly shifted simply by promoting bicycle circulation. For some, the adoption of alternative mobility was a performative consequence of the bicycle being more efficient. For others, the bicycle was mainly an object serving the environmental cause. Once those various instances connect on the pivotal element of the bicycle taking various component positions—object, performance, belief, value—a paradigm towards modern mobilities is more likely to occur.

A word on the values component of a paradigm. The various actors in society may believe that they act according to certain values. For instance, activists may expect that major transitions would occur by aligning values system-wide. However, it has long been suggested that collectives may perform without shared meaning or goals—a paradigm perspective does not assume the existence and the exact role of a shared value(s) component, especially since those may operate at various levels of the structure, that is, individual, group, and society.

Indeed, a paradigm perspective suggests that ambiguous—or even counterfactual—*beliefs* may nevertheless lead to positively valued collective performance which could then form the basis to develop a system of collective action. In Figure 3.1, we exemplify the nuance of a traditional naïve view of paradigms, centred on value, whereby realistic paradigms occur by recombination of elements whose value may not be shared.

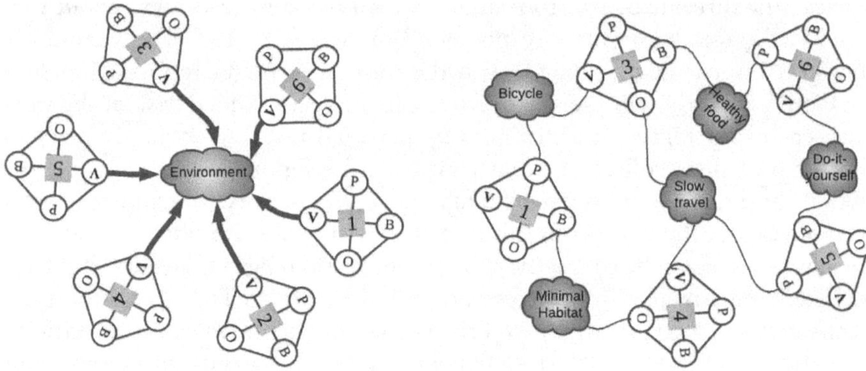

Figure 3.1 Two models of paradigms: naïve versus realistic

Note: Popular conceptions assume that paradigm function of a central value, hence transition, should be approached by making the environment the central value of society. However, paradigms function by meshing local instances of individuals who may differ on their (V)alues, (B)eliefs, (O)bjects, and (P)erformance. Their interactions occur on elements that may not even play a similar role for each individual.

(a) When considering ecological transition, one may imagine environment as the ultimate shared value.
(b) A realistic target paradigm may not function as such, and it may occur by relying on a fine meshing of individual instances: bicycle being valued by some (e.g. individual 3) and being just a work for others (1); minimal habitat as being viewed more efficient by some (1), as being convenient and cheap by others (4); slow travel as being valued by some (4) and a local work for others (5) and just a mean of transportation of the rest (3); healthy food as medical imperative by some (3) and a production by others (6); do it yourself practices as being a pleasure by some (6); the foundation of an industrial system by others (5); etc.

The dynamics to an ecological transition

The wish for a shift towards environmental sustainability requires developing sets of beliefs where all components of an expected future paradigm fit together and lead to the enactment of an environmentally sustainable society. This doesn't mean plastering values all around, as the ultimately revealed value matters more than the transitory and locally espoused ones.

What if the seemingly large and threatening ecological transition, for example, were performed by meshing various esthetical changes (e.g. replacing the emotional love of a car-centric lifestyle by the love of a bike-centric lifestyle, so that the population willingly accept to renounce toxic practices)? Here we targeted CO_2-emitting vehicles, but it can similarly be applied to over-consumption of meat, to plane transportation, to fast fashion, etc. This could enable the overcoming of ecological anxiety and its subsequent troubling political backlash, where populist politicians, in denial of climate change, seduce the population by promising them to just ignore the threat of the future and enjoy life as we know it.

Another conceptual obstacle to paradigm evolutions lies in their competing with each other and even exhibiting significant incompatibility. Regarding ecological transition, paradigmatic tension has already been identified, for instance around the issues of nuclear energy or economic growth. Environmentally conscious activists, for example, may all wish for an ecological transition—a concern that is increasingly shared by the population at large—and yet they end up falling into clear sub-paradigms with different perspectives on the transition. For instance, some activists consider that ecological transition can only be approached by rejecting nuclear power and find themselves opposed to others holding a paradigm that nuclear power may be an interesting tool to decarbonize the economy. A similar paradigm tension occurs between those who consider ecological transition as requiring to reject growth and capitalism, as opposed to those for which a capitalist and growth economy may be compatible with a more respectful future.

All in all, the ecological transition can be expected to occur in a series of phase transitions—that is, a paradigm shift. Yet the transition may neither require global alignment—as it can occur by a cascade of paradigm shifts at lower levels—nor require overarching agreement—as an ecological paradigm might exist without explicit value alignment.

This possibility does not exonerate us from attempting to align as many stakeholders as possible. It only provides more options for collective action regarding an issue that desperately needs progress. A rich system of beliefs and practices must be elaborated to prevent our current unsustainable societal paradigm from dominating over desirable alternatives. Similarly, work must be done to defuse the paradigmatic tensions among the various alternatives, be it support for nuclear energy or the growth economy, towards ecological transition. The careful analysis and reckoning of these apparent paradigmatic incompatibilities might be necessary to progress towards a pragmatic and effective ecological transition.

Food for thought:

- How would you describe your own instance of our current climate-threatening paradigm? What values, beliefs, and practices do you currently hold that prevent you to accomplish a shift at your local level?
- Given that paradigm shift is not a smooth process (and indeed it can be painful for various stakeholders), which successive phases of change would you consider? Can you identify the pains you can anticipate and how you could mitigate them by constructing new aesthetics? Break down the problem into sub-problems such as transportation versus food versus housing.
- Given the differing interests, values, and beliefs of the various players (e.g. businesses, consumers, energy providers), how could these phases be tailored to reduce conflict as much as possible? Think of any win-wins that could be implemented.
- Translate the parable of the stonecutters and the cathedral of the medieval society paradigm, into our modern time, to think of what a future paradigm of *sustainability* could be. In that future, think of examples of three distinct citizens interacting in that paradigm and how their role and the meanings they provide may function around pivotal objects and practices? (e.g. bicycle or cooking at home).

Related research

Cavarretta, F. (2021). On the hard problem of selecting bundles of rules: A conceptual exploration of heuristic emergence processes. *Management Decision*, *9*(7), 1598–1616.

Cavarretta, F. (2022). Paradigm, doctrines, etc.: A grammar of social action. In ESSEC (Ed.), *Working paper*.

Cavarretta, F., & Furr, N. (wp10). An inquiry into the epistemic properties of entrepreneurs' keystone rules. *ESSEC Working Knowledge/SSRN eLibrary*.

Note

1 See Cavarretta (2022) for more details.

Part II

Sustainability

The need for transparency and accountability

4 In search of a compass for navigating the ecological transition

Adrian Zicari

In this collective book *Navigating the Ecological Transition*, this chapter intends to provide a reflection on the compass we need for that navigation. This travel is not a comfortable coastal navigation (i.e., the land on one side, and the sea on the other), where references are clear and straightforward. It is instead a kind of adventurous, challenging navigation without sight of the land, without maps, without GPS. This is a journey to a *terra incognita*—to a place nobody has been before.

Part of the challenge lies in that the ongoing ecological transition means not only a change in ways of life (i.e., consume less, buy local, recycle), but it also means changes in business models (i.e., the three "re-"—reuse, remanufacture, recycle). Moreover, it means a radical change in mindsets, the acknowledgment that nature is not infinite, that the planet has limits, and that we have already trespassed some of those limits.

In this context, the choice of an appropriate compass is a key issue. A misaligned, broken or defective compass would lead us to catastrophe. As such, it is important to reflect on which kind of compass companies need nowadays for this perilous navigation. It is clear that this kind of navigation system has to be based, or at least related, with Accounting. This makes sense, as Accounting provides entrepreneurs, managers and investors with feedback on how their businesses operate and how healthy they are. Consequently, the following provides a reflection on how accounting practices and reports could evolve to become better guides for companies in this challenging ecological transition.

Accounting and its limits

Accounting has a long history. Benedetto Cottrugli and Fra Luca Paccioli first described its conceptual basis, the double-entry system, during the Renaissance. At the time, the purpose of accounting was managerial, that is, to provide useful information to merchants operating in Mediterranean ports (Zicari, 2022). While merchants would occasionally partner for a commercial project—for example, a long voyage—there were no external investors, and consequently no reporting to third parties. All accounting information

DOI: 10.4324/9781003522355-6

was internal, for decision-making purposes. Furthermore, both for Cottrugli and for Paccioli, Accounting was not an isolated practice, devoid of ethical considerations. Accounting was for them a necessary practice for the respectable merchant. Indeed, both authors (who were devout Catholics) insisted that merchants should do their business according to a coherent set of ethical values. They would have recoiled at the idea of accounting as a mere technical tool, with a logic of its own.

With the passage of time (indeed, several centuries), the role of external investors increased. Moreover, large companies, no longer individual merchants, became the central actor of economic life, and, consequently, Accounting became more and more oriented to these very providers of capital, the key readers of accounting reports. Furthermore, ethical considerations were gradually overlooked in the context of Accounting, the exception perhaps being for Forensic Accounting. As such, nowadays the person in the street tends to identify Accounting with accounting reports, which are normally called *financial reports*. "Financial" because it is oriented to financers.

Without entering into technicalities, one may present contemporary financial accounting as oriented to the preparation of two main reports: the Balance Sheet and the Profit and Loss Statement (P&L). Of course, there are other reports, but one may safely focus on these two as the most relevant to our analysis. The Balance Sheet is a description and a quantification of what the company has and what the company owes. Logically, the more the company has and the less the company owes, the better. The P&L explains what the company did during a certain period (a quarter, a year): how much it sold, the different costs, and as a consequence, the bottom line. The more money in the bottom line, the better. Together, these documents are taken-for-granted representations of what the company has and what the company does.

One may see that both reports share some similar traits. First, there is no notion of limit. There is never *enough*. One may argue that the achievement of an organizational mission—for example, for a hospital, to cure patients—would require some financial means, and that it is fair to measure whether those means are there or not. Once those necessary financial means achieved, that would be enough. However, the logic of conventional financial statements omits this consideration. What were formally the financial means to an objective became an objective in itself. The greater the financial results, the better. The sky's the limit.

Second, the viewpoint of these reports is that of financers. The bottom line, what one calls the *results*, is results for shareholders only. Other stakeholders benefit from the economic activity of the company—for example, employees and the State—but those contributions are not clearly stated in the P&L. Third, the results considered are the economic results, while the environmental and social consequences of the firm's activities are overlooked. These latter impacts could eventually find their way into economic results—for instance, environmental fines—but this remains an exception, not the rule.

One may see that these criticisms do not point to the quality of the reports. Indeed, they are precisely the kind of reports our students learn about in our school, as is the case in any business school in the world. An innumerable amount of companies all over the world regularly produce these reports, which are in many cases audited by respectable and serious professionals, following world class standards. As such, it is not that these reports are faulty or imperfect. It is that they omit important information—the kind of information that matters for navigating the ecological transition.

Some initiatives to account for the social and environmental dimensions

Fortunately, there have been many initiatives to improve the situation. Following Burritt and Schaltegger (2010), one can present these initiatives as either "inside-out" or "outside-in". "Inside-out" initiatives attempt to develop ecological and social indicators inside of the firm. This is a central issue, as managers need to understand what happens in the organizations they lead.

One may imagine that managers are aware of what is going on in terms of environmental and social performance, but this is not necessarily the case. For instance, Durden (2006) presents the case study of a small company in New Zealand whose owner, founder and top manager was an enthusiastic proponent of CSR. Despite his best intentions, the company failed to deploy a CSR strategy, and middle managers ended up using conventional indicators. Gond et al. (2012) contrast between a conventional management control system and a set of sustainability indicators. They explore several situations where the control system and the sustainability indicators are more or less integrated, pointing to the challenges (and the promise) of such an integration.

Most of the initiatives and studies in sustainability and accounting look today at the "outside-in" perspective, that is, at the reporting of social and environmental impacts. There is no scarcity of new reporting models. And without being exhaustive, several reporting models necessarily have to be mentioned.

First is the Global Reporting Initiative (GRI), an initiative of the United Nations and a group of investors. The GRI created a wide, encompassing, comprehensive set of indicators, covering a broad range of economic, environmental and social impacts. These indicators were selected and regularly updated by means of a participatory methodology that involves many stakeholders all over the world. Many companies nowadays prepare their sustainability reports following the GRI guidelines. Second, the Sustainability Accounting Standard Board (SASB), now in collaboration with the International Integrated Reporting Council. Simplifying a bit, one may say that the SASB model is more focused on shareholders, that is, on the financial translation of environmental and social risks. Third, the Corporate Sustainability

Reporting Directive (CSRD), a rule created by the European Union. Other initiatives exist, and possibly others still will be created in the future. Thus, there is no consensus about a shared standard for sustainability accounting.

Without entering into technicalities, two aspects are worth mentioning here. First is the idea of *materiality*, a buzzword among my fellow accountants that can be replaced by "relevant". In this light, a discussion about materiality is a discussion about what matters in a report—what information should be included, and what information can be safely omitted, as it would not be *material* (i.e., relevant).

However, materiality is not an abstract concept. Something is material to somebody. In the case of the GRI model, materiality corresponds to the planet and to society. That is, the impact of the company's actions to the planet and to society. Financial implications of those impacts are not in the picture of GRI. For the SASB instead, materiality corresponds to the viewpoint of shareholders, that is, how environmental and social issues impact company value. Environmental and social issues with no financial implications are not in the picture of SASB. Finally, the CSRD covers the impacts of the company on the planet and on society and, on the other side, the environmental and social impacts on the company value. This combined perspective is called *double materiality*. As an example of double materiality, the carbon emissions of a company impact the planet, while climate change as a whole creates logistical risks for the same company, with a consequent impact on corporate value. A single materiality approach would only focus only on one part, either the impact on the planet and society (e.g., GRI) or the impact of the planet and society on the company's value (e.g., SASB).

Another point is the elusive cause-to-consequence relation. Michel Porter and Claas van der Linde theoretically argued in a 1995 issue of the Harvard Business Review that there would be win-win opportunities in which companies improve both environmental performance and financial results. This is what one nowadays calls eco-efficiency—the improvement of industrial processes and achieving more output with less pollution. More recently, in a 2012 issue of the *Management Accounting Research* journal, Jean-Pascal Gond et al. assume that successful sustainability management can lead to higher corporate performance. However, there is no definitive proof for that relation.

Of course, in some cases, being greener can imply better results. Perhaps not in some others. Too many factors are at play: type of industrial sector, competition, corporate strategy, macroeconomic factors, and so on. As such, the relation between sustainability performance and profits, whether positive or not, is not clear. As we accountants like to say, "it depends". In this sense, Integrated Reporting and now SASB have the merit of having attempted to explore this cause-to-consequence relation, trying to elaborate on how a company deploys its business model and links its environmental and social issues with financial results. However, the perspective of the planet and society is better addressed by GRI, while CSRD intends to address both sides of the question.

The Value-Added Statement

This chapter would not be complete without mention of the Value-Added Statement (VAS), a reporting tool that I have been exploring in my research. Without entering into too much detail, the VAS represents the activities of a company during a certain period (similarly to the Profit and Loss Statement). But differently from the P&L, the VAS explicates how much of the economic value created is shared among different stakeholders, most notably employees, financers, the State (taxes), community (donations) and the company itself (reserves for reinvestment). Based on the same information already existing in the company's accounting systems, the VAS presents the results differently, with a fresh perspective. By doing so, the VAS provides a completely different view of the company, showing that the result of economic value is shared among different categories or groups of persons.

This latter consideration is far from arithmetical. Indeed, it contrasts with the implicit logic of the Profit & Loss Statement, which suggests that costs are bad (i.e., they have to be reduced) and that the bottom line is good (i.e., it has to be increased). This simplistic logic is consistent with the 1970 Ed Friedman admonition to managers, preaching that "the social responsibility of business is to increase its profits".

Instead, in the VAS, each stakeholder receives part of the economic value created. There is no *a priori* mandate to increase or diminish any of the distributions. The extreme simplification of the bottom line is replaced by a clarification—an explication of how the pie is created and distributed among the involved parties. Paolo Quattrone (2020) contends that the use of VAS opens the door for negotiations and a continuous redefinition of the company's priorities among stakeholders. He claims that the extensive use of the VAS in post-war Italy was one of the causes of the economic miracle in that country.

Use of the VAS

There have been many attempts to use VAS. Perhaps the most known episode corresponds to the Corporate Report (ASSC, 1975), a white paper prepared by the British accounting profession. It was a visionary document that merits to be read today, and a reflection on the purpose, challenges and promise of corporate reporting. The document proposed that the VAS should be part of the mandatory set of reports of any company, saying that several audiences (beyond investors) "have a reasonable right to be informed . . . by corporate reports". Despite this strong endorsement, the VAS did not become mandatory, and even if many companies disclosed it on a voluntary basis, its use eventually waned. There were many reasons for this failure, and Burchell et al. (1985) points to a "constellation" of factors, some of them of political nature. In a similar vein, Pong and Mitchell (2005) also contend that the disclosures proposed by the VAS were resisted by company managers.

There have been other initiatives, in several parts of the world, including Italy, Germany and South Africa. In each case, a different model was created. Moreover, the GRI model, among a large collection of indicators, includes the "Disclosure 201-1—Direct economic value generated and distributed". For the moment, there is no standardization, which of course makes comparability difficult and possibly diminishes the reliability of these reports.

In my case, I have been working with a particular VAS model, created by the former partner of a Big Four firm in Latin America. The story of how this model was created has been presented elsewhere (Zicari & Perera Aldama, 2020), but perhaps the most important issue is the active involvement of a high-level practitioner who creates and implements a social reporting model in many companies. The model has been quite successful and to this day, more than 20 large companies in several countries in the region use it. Some of these companies are incipient *multilatinas*, that is, multinational firms headquartered in Latin America. In some cases, these firms represent a sizeable part of the GDP of their home country. I also took part in qualitative study that explored how managers take the information of VAS reports into consideration, and how they make decisions based on them (Perera Aldama & Zicari, 2012).

VAS reports can be used for comparative purposes. For instance, Pinto and Souza Ribeiro (2004) compare the social performance of different industrial companies in the Santa Catarina state in Brazil. This comparison was possible because there is a local VAS model, frequently used in the country, which has become mandatory for firms quoted on the stock exchange. The comparison can also be longitudinal—over time—and this is possible when the same company has consistently reported with the same model. This is, for instance, the case of a large mining firm in Mexico that has now been using this model for more than 15 years. In my study with Perera Aldama in 2017, we identify a consistent pattern of distribution to employees over a decade (Zicari & Perera Aldama, 2017). As the company increased its created value in the long run, employees received a substantial part of that created value. But curiously, employees were not impacted by the global economic volatility the company faces. As the price of metals—being a commodity—can rapidly change in the international markets, it is frequent for a mining firm to have fatter or leaner years according to the rise and fall in the price of metals. Nevertheless, the employee share of the value crated by the company was not impacted during the negative years, and it was the shareholders who diminished their dividends to compensate. In the long run, both parties in this case—employees and shareholders—benefit. Only that employees were protected from the vicissitudes of the international markets for metals. This case shows how the VAS can explain a social policy that is consistently maintained over many years. And of course, this has been only a partial aspect of the VAS—the distribution of economic value—that has to be complemented by the analysis of other elements, such as the environment.

Accounting—with a purpose

This chapter has hoped to provide some reflections on the tools companies would need for the navigation toward an ecological transition. In particular, I have commented on several existing international initiatives, pointing to some of their promises and challenges. And finally, an explanation of a particular tool, the Value-Added Statement, and a presentation of its potential use and benefits.

Challenging as this environmental transition is, one can be confident in that some tools stemming from or developed from accounting practices can be of help. Together with other tools coming from other disciplines, Accounting can provide some of them that managers need for this purpose.

Key takeaways:

- Any journey into sustainability must bear in mind accounting: It provides entrepreneurs, managers and investors with feedback on how their businesses operate and how healthy they are.
- Early accounting focused on internal usage and for providing useful information for decision-making purposes. However, Benedetto Cottrugli and Fra Luca Paccioli insisted that merchants should do their business according to a coherent set of ethical values.
- As the role of external investors increased, Accounting became a tool that was increasingly oriented to these very providers of capital, the key readers of accounting reports.
- Today, Accounting is identified with accounting reports, which are normally called *financial reports*. "Financial" because it is oriented to financers.
- Contemporary financial accounting basically generates the Balance Sheet—a description and a quantification of what the company has and what the company owes—and the Profit and Loss Statement (P&L)—what the company did during a certain period (a quarter, a year): how much it sold, the different costs, and as a consequence, the bottom line.
- These reports omit important information for navigating the ecological transition.
- Among sustainability reports, three stand out: The GRI featuring a comprehensive set of indicators, covering a broad range of economic, environmental and social impacts. The SASB in collaboration with the International Integrated Reporting Council, more focused on shareholders and the financial translation of environmental and social risks. And the CSRD, which intends to address both sides of the question.
- An alternative way of sustainability accounting is the VAS (Value-Added Statement) that explicates how much of the economic value created is shared among different stakeholders, most notably employees, financers, the State (taxes), community (donations) and the company itself (reserves for reinvestment).

- The VAS provides a completely different view of the company, showing that the result of economic value is shared among different categories or groups of persons.

Food for thought:

- Accounting has a cliché of being sober and dreary. How is this cliché wrong? And to what extent are accountants superheroes?
- Think of your school, company or organization. If you were to conduct a VAS, how do they contribute to the wider, common good?
- Some critics contend that social and environmental reporting can be used for greenwashing purposes. To what extent is this true? And false?

References

Accounting Standards Steering Committee. (1975). *The corporate report*. Author.

Burchell, S., Clubb, C., & Hopwood, A. (1985). Accounting in its social context: Towards a history of value added in the United Kingdom. *Accounting, Organizations and Society*, *10*(4), 381–413.

Burritt, R., & Schaltegger, S. (2010). Sustainability accounting and reporting: Fad or trend? *Accounting, Auditing and Accountability Journal*, *23*(7), 829–846.

Durden, C. (2006). Towards a socially responsible management control system. *Accounting, Auditing & Accountability Journal*, *21*(5), 671–694.

Friedman, M. (1970). The social responsibility of business is to increase its profits. *The New York Times Magazine*.

Gond, J. P., Grubnic, S., Herzig, C., & Moon, J. (2012). Configuring management control systems: Theorizing the integration of strategy and sustainability. *Management Accounting Research*, *23*(3), 205–223.

Perera Aldama, L., & Zicari, A. (2012). Value-added reporting as a tool for sustainability: A Latin American experience. *Corporate Governance: The International Journal of Business in Society*, *12*(4), 485–498.

Pinto, A., & Ribeiro, M. (2004). Balanço social: avaliacao de informacoes fornecidas por empresas industriais situadas no estado de Santa Catarina. *Revista Contabilidade & Finanças, USP, Sao Paulo*, *36*, 21–34.

Pong, C., & Mitchell, F. (2005). Accounting for disappearance: A contribution to the history of the value added statement in the UK. *Accounting Historians Journal*, *32*(2), 173–199.

Porter, M., & van der Linde, C. (1995). Green and competitive: Ending the stalemate. *Harvard Business Review*, *73*(5), 120–134.

Quattrone, P. (2020). A smart third way. *Developing Leaders*, *36*, 66–74.

Zicari, A. (2022). Bringing inspiration from the past: A renaissance manual for merchants. In L. Biggiero, D. de Jongh, B. Priddat, J. Wieland, A. Zicari, & D. Fischer (Eds.), *The relational view of economics* (1st ed., pp. 97–110). Springer.

Zicari, A., & Perera Aldama, L. (2017). Value-added statements as a communication tool for stakeholders: The case of Industrias Peñoles in Mexico. In E. Freeman, J. Kujala, & S. Sachs (Eds.), *Stakeholder engagement: Clinical research cases* (pp. 193–214). Springer.

Zicari, A., & Perera Aldama, L. (2020). Building from scratch: An auto-ethnographic approach for the development of a social reporting model. *Social and Environmental Accountability Journal*, *40*(2), 101–115.

5 Animal welfare

How sustainability accounting can trigger awareness and positive change?[1]

Mark Christensen and Geoffrey Lamberton

In past years, corporate responsibility, sustainability and, more recently, the concept of conscious business have brought the importance of ethical business to the forefront. Companies are henceforth expected to take into account the impact of their operations on their employees, suppliers, consumers, communities, and the planet—and act responsibly towards them. As the notion of a sustainable, responsible organization gains traction, so does the idea that humankind is inherently connected with the biosphere as a whole, including that other aspect of the family of things, those fellow sentient beings that inhabit the planet—animals.

Why should we and, more relevantly for this book, businesses be concerned? For one, business operations concern the environment, including the sentient beings living in that environment. Moreover, the food chain necessarily includes firms that deal directly with animals. Take an example from Faunalytics (https://faunalytics.org), which provides access to research and analysis of animal issues. According to the non-profit, 293.2 million cattle were slaughtered in 2020 to end up on our supermarket shelves. The same goes for sheep, UN data for 2016 citing 550 million as the yearly number slaughtered to fill markets worldwide. In this light, it is an ethical requirement that corporations ensure the decent treatment of these creatures as they are reared and fed into the slaughterhouse for consumption.

Indeed, there is increasing acceptance that humans have no moral right to cause other species undue or unacceptable levels of suffering, much of it caused by the view that animals are humankind's renewable resources without inherent value. Embedded in our culture and strengthened over generations, this leads to us making a sort of trade-off between animal suffering and the benefits they bring us—food. The argument goes that animal suffering is unfortunate, but in the end run, we, as humans, are more important. However, under pressure from animal rights activist campaigns, some countries have enforced laws which ban some of the more brutal practices which cause "undue suffering". One example is that of the debeaking of poultry and extreme confinement. The problem is that the consumer is most often spared the psychological impact of witnessing animal suffering due to the fact that farming and slaughtering facilities are

DOI: 10.4324/9781003522355-7

physically far from the consumer's plate. Can ethical accounting help alleviate animal suffering and contribute to improving animal welfare in our farming industries? We think so (Christensen & Lamberton, 2021).

The case of Australian live sheep export (LSE)

On the west coast of Australia, it is common to witness multi-deck, purpose-built ships being loaded with sheep—roughly 70,000 of them—destined for the Middle East. At its peak in 1988, this industry—LSE—transported 7.1 million ovine in what has been termed the world's largest migration of animals. The voyage, more than 10,000 kilometres, is strenuous and characterized by high temperatures, cramped living space, lack of light, high levels of mechanical noise and the constant vibration of the ship's engines. Outbreaks of disease in such conditions are frequent.

Those in support of live sheep export claim that the industry has economic value and allows for the required Halal slaughtering to take place offshore. While LSE is profitable for the exporters and ensures reasonable selling prices to sheep farmers, the industry's turnover has been in decline since 2005, its market share shrinking to 11% and replaced by providers closer to Middle Eastern markets. Concerning animal welfare, research has shown the Australian LSE to be unsustainable from a social perspective due to frequent cases of cruelty to animals brought to light by activists and the media. Neighbouring New Zealand, also a producer of sheep, introduced regulation for live sheep export in 2007 and the practice has since ceased due to risk of the country's reputation as a responsible exporter. Australia, however, continues its trade despite repeated cycles of scandal and public outcry.

The situation seems to be one of two disconnected worlds. On the one hand, animals are seen as production units in an industry focused essentially on economic returns, and on the other animals are viewed as beings with feelings and emotions—with rights to be treated ethically by humans. The fact that the trade has continued for over 30 years leads us to conclude that animals are seen as an asset on the balance sheet that require being converted into revenue.

What of public outcry? From previous research, we identified a cyclic occurrence of events that we term scandal-reaction-obduracy. Typically, the process runs through a loop: first, a case of cruelty to animals is exposed, or the large-scale painful death of animals during a journey. This is followed by public outcry, with government reaction that condemns the event but refraining from pointing blame. An enquiry into the event is often launched and subsequent changes in legislation are brought into effect that, although enforced by the LSE industry, have little effect in improving the welfare and conditions that the sheep endure. Invariably, public interest and outcry fade away and the industry continues to refuse to change its ways despite widespread public distrust in the effect of LSE regulations.

Indeed, over the years, protest, petitions, bills in Parliament, and media coverage of the scandals have not succeeded in making sustainability the meeting point of any attempt to negotiate with the various stakeholders to improve the situation. On their side, LSE stakeholders have retorted with campaigns to soften their image among the public with websites offering such calls to action as "meet the farmers" and "get the facts". It looks probable that the cycle of scandal-reaction-obduracy will continue.

In this current stalemate, we propose action that will—if not lead to the banning of LSE—at least raise awareness and provide a tool for measurement and improvement of animal welfare in the industry. In essence, it gives animals a presence in sustainability accounting and draws on practices that use a range of indicators to gain a more complete comprehension of the social, environmental, and animal welfare aspects of performance for those working in the LSE industry—as well as a wider range of stakeholders unable to grasp the conditions on board the export ships. We call it the Animal Welfare Account, or AWA.

Our hope is that the AWA will go beyond simple numbers and cost-benefits that the current accounting framework gives, to provide information that will lead to empathy for sentient creatures subject to fear and pain. It will simultaneously serve as a tool to review and improve management practices in the LSE industry. Theoretically, it should also offer awareness to those in the LSE supply chain and an understanding of the suffering that sheep undergo when being shipped to slaughter 10,000 kilometres away from their grazing grounds. All in all, the bottom line of the AWA is for it to give a deep account that morally links the account users to the sufferer in a way that will lead to social action to remove that suffering.

Table 5.1 Measurable animal welfare performance indicators (adapted from Wickham et al., 2015)

Five domains of animal welfare + contextual factors	*Welfare performance indicators*
Nutrition	**Feed consumption and access** **Water consumption and access** **Body condition scoring (tick box)** **Gut fill scoring (tick box)** **Body weight**
Environment (comfort)	**Daily temperature in pens** • Wet bulb temp • Dry bulb temp • Ambient temp **Humidity** **Ventilation** **Stock density** **Respiration and panting—breathing or panting scores (discrete scales—slow, medium, fast, extreme)** **Noise level**

(*Continued*)

Table 5.1 (Continued)

Five domains of animal welfare + contextual factors	*Welfare performance indicators*
	Lighting—brightness and duration (hours per day) Condition of pad Ability to lie down Bedding Ammonia Carbon dioxide (CO_2)
Health	Mortality rates, including cause of death Morbidity—incidence and type of diseases Haematological measures from veterinarian interventions Animal slips and falls and resulting injuries Number of lambs born Number of abortions Number of pregnant sheep and estimated stage of pregnancy
Behaviour	Qualitative behaviour assessment involving: • comfortable/uncomfortable; • alert/responsive; • calm/sleepy; • rumination rate and indications of inanition; • shivering
Mental state	Qualitative behaviour assessment – happy, sad, anxious, relaxed, nervous, frightened Erratic behaviour, including self-harm and aggression.
Contextual factors	Qualifications of staff Certification of stockpersons in low stress handling Number of vets on board Weather conditions

The live sheep export industry: a sustainable future?

The task is not easy. For the Animal Welfare Account to have an impact, it will need to trigger the desired benefits to the wider community of stakeholders while overcoming resistance within the LSE industry itself. Opposition is likely, notably because the implementation of AWA will necessarily carry with it additional costs to the trade, both capital and recurrent. AWA implies changes throughout the journey, especially in light of the fact that current practices are incapable of extracting reliable data for most of the indicators included in the above AWA table. These are

- increasing the number of approved veterinarians travelling on board each LSE shipment from the current level of one per ship to one per deck (meaning between 9 and 11 veterinarians per journey);

- altering accommodation for veterinarians on board the LSE ships, thus reduce space for sheep;
- installing wireless telemetric measuring equipment on each deck and in multiple places;
- reducing stocking densities so as to allow inspection of the flocks as well as increasing sheep welfare;
- increasing record-keeping and report preparation.

Given that the fixed costs of an LSE journey vastly outstrip the variable costs, exporters will be inclined to maximize the number of sheep per square metre before considering other factors. But there remain several pertinent financial and non-financial arguments that might turn the situation around.

First is disinvestment. The effective implementation of AWAs necessarily engenders changes to the ships and their staffing. This will decrease margins for the exporters with predicted profits reaching a mere 10%—enough to turn a potential investor away from supporting LSE activities. Second, AWAs can also appeal to shareholder activists and politicians who have no allegiance to the LSE industry, both able to bring pressure to call for reinforced legislation. As in the case of New Zealand, increased legislation may result in increasingly eroded profit margins, thus adding pressure to the industry to change from its old ways towards a more sustainable new.

The fact that sheep rearing is increasingly being located closer to the Middle Eastern market for sheep export might also trigger change—or at least a need for AWA to be diligently implemented. These new locations also require sea transport, and it seems probable that Australian exporters will displace their ships to these destinations to carry out shorter and more frequent journeys to their markets—thus reducing the financial incentive to overcrowd on board pens.

The fact that New Zealand introduced policy in favour of choosing to withdraw from LSE means that Australia can follow suit. The basis for action requires tools such as the AWA which take into account non-financial disclosure of factors liked to animal welfare. For in matters regarding the suffering of sentient beings, conventional accounting methods are virtually useless.

Furthermore, an essential area is that of animal welfare activists. Despite their actions, the Australian LSE industry has managed to survive decades of scandals related to cruelty on animals and degrading conditions of their transportation to the slaughterhouse. These activists need to be informed and trained on their understanding of what a sustainable LSE industry looks like. Research and academia can play a role here as voice able to offer a mediating middle ground, supported by data and measurement as offered by the AWA. And this in an attempt to both raise awareness of the utility of the LSE industry, highlight the threat to Australia's reputation on the international stage, and push for an ethical and sustainable approach to the treatment of animals concerned by it.

Sustainability needs to become the focus of any talks and changes in the industry. And not just from those fighting against it for animal welfare.

The commitment and engagement around sustainability of those working in LSE is also essential. In addition, and in line with Actor-Network-Theory (ANT), if sustainability is to be considered in its fullest sense, not only people will have an active role, but non-human entities—objects, ideas, processes, and any other relevant factors—must be seen as just as important in finding a solution. This necessarily means including the animals concerned, the ships, and the seas over which LSE journeys.

Sustainability accounting through the AWA is feasible, able to be prepared for each journey and by each company. The additional costs related to this will very likely cause resistance, in which case changes to the legislation will be necessary to incite the LSE industry to accommodate it. In the end run, the future of LSE, in the light of our arguments in this chapter, looks likely to be faced with two alternatives: conversion to full sustainability or a ceasing of its activities along the lines of LSE in New Zealand.

Sustainability must necessarily include the removal of all suffering for animals. And here, it is relevant to point out that what is considered unnecessary or unacceptable suffering is largely determined within the public domain, or by consumer demand. If those concerned—from the LSE industry to the consumer—are to make informed moral choices, the need an understanding of the impact of their decisions. This includes the suffering in the journey it takes to get the product and the profit to its destination. The AWA, if implemented, will provide this much-needed visibility on animal welfare.

Key takeaways:

- There is increasing acceptance that humans have no moral right to cause other species undue or unacceptable levels of suffering, much of it caused by the view that animals are humankind's renewable resources without inherent value.
- The Live Sheep Export industry in Australia has come under repeated criticism for its lack of concern for animal welfare.
- At its peak in 1988, Australian LSE transported 7.1 million ovine in what has been termed the world's largest migration of animals.
- The voyage, more than 10,000 kilometres, is characterized by high temperatures, cramped living space, lack of light, high levels of mechanical noise and constant vibration of the ship's engines. Outbreaks of disease in such conditions are frequent.
- There exists a scandal-reaction-obduracy process, whereby public outcry causes government condemnation, slight changes in legislation with no impact on the industry, a fading of public outcry, and the refusal of the industry to change.
- The Animal Welfare Account (AWA) proposes a comprehensive framework to measure animal welfare performance by bridging the gap between viewing animals as economic assets and recognizing their sentience, fostering empathy and driving social action for improving animal welfare.

- The implementation of such a tool will mean additional costs to the LSE industry—and very likely resistance.
- This can be overcome by introducing tighter legislation, re-orienting activist understanding, and bringing the various stakeholders together with sustainability as the focus to make positive change.
- Two scenarios confront the future of LSE in Australia: conversion to full sustainability or a ceasing of its activities along the lines of LSE in New Zealand.

Food for thought:

- What about animal welfare in your country? Has it become a feature of CSR policies for companies? To what extent has government legislation tackled the issue?
- To what extent do you support the rights of animals as sentient beings? Why? What made you think this way? And have your eating habits changed as a result?
- Is animal welfare necessarily a topic for the privileged in developed economies to embrace? What would be a possible standpoint from those in developing or emerging economies? Or to what extent is it a universal issue to be concerned about?
- After reading this chapter, how have your opinions about accounting changed?

Note

1 From an interview with Tom Gamble, Executive Director, Council on Business & Society.

References

Christensen, M., & Lamberton, G. (2021). Accounting for animal welfare: Addressing epistemic vices during live sheep export voyages. *Journal of Business Ethics*. Advance online publication. https://doi.org/10.1007/s10551-021-04857-6

Wickham, S., Collins, T., Barnes, A., Miller, D., Beatty, D., Stockman, C., Blache, D., Wemelsfelder, F., & Fleming, T. (2015). Validating the use of qualitative behavioural assessment as a measure of the welfare of sheep during transport. *Journal of Applied Animal Welfare Science*, *18*, 269–286.

6 From anti-greenwashing toolbox to EU leadership's sword

Geneviève Helleringer

The imperative to mitigate climate change and accelerate low-carbon transition has recently achieved results that only very few would have bet on half a decade ago. Shareholders have put pressure on oil titans.[1] Institutional investors, under the pressure of pension funds and sovereign wealth funds, have largely removed fossil energy from their portfolios. Even courts have taken strong stances at the request of activists.[2] While the mobilization is striking, and the energy to overcome collective action problems remarkable, there has been a concern about false advertising in the marketing of supposedly "green" products. Mere pretended concern about the environment, or "greenwashing", tends to undermine the low-carbon transition objective. There has been growing scrutiny since evidence that companies routinely engage in greenwashing.

An example of "*greenwashing*" occurred in the energy industry when the companies Shell, Total, and Eni sold their stake in the Umuechem oil field in Nigeria in 2021. This divestment appeared and was presented as an effort to clean up and green their activities.[3] The public was under the impression that energy companies could clean up their operations and obtain funds to invest in new, low-emission business lines. However, after the sale to a private-equity backed firm, Trans-Niger Oil & Gas, the level of high-emission burning of excess gas released when pumping up oil at the Umuechem oil field quadrupled.[4] In other words, overall emissions increased rather than decreased: the dirty assets were merely shifted around and made even dirtier in the process.[5]

Against the backdrop of what looks like a market failure, the political sphere is expected to play a central role in making changes with no regard for private interests. Accordingly, pressure to address environmental concerns has featured highly in European Union (EU) policy, with the European Green Deal[6] of December 2019 supporting long-term green investments, and the proposed European Climate Law as a framework for achieving climate neutrality.[7] In particular, the European Commission has adopted an Action Plan on Financing Sustainable Growth,[8] which aims to reorient capital flows towards sustainable investment and to foster transparency and long-termism. The Action Plan has engendered three Regulations—"Disclosure",[9] "Benchmark",[10] and "Taxonomy"[11]—between 2019 and 2021, as well as a recent draft Directive on Corporate Sustainability Due Diligence.[12]

DOI: 10.4324/9781003522355-8

The *raison d'être* of these developments is rooted in the following conundrum: how can investors assess whether a particular investment is sustainable? Asking the target companies risks being misled, since companies are keen to appear green. Information intermediaries provide sustainability assessments with large variance for the same company, this dispersion often reflecting differences in the assessment method. Investors may be ill-equipped to form their own view, for want of data, expertise, or time. A public intervention therefore seems warranted. It is therefore not surprising that the European Commission concluded that a regulatory standard was necessary to provide a clear definition and taxonomy of what economic activity counts as "sustainable".

While the toolbox has quickly expanded, a closer observation of the instruments reveals that some might be blunter than hoped. The mechanics of these instruments might also reveal a post-Brexit style in EU legislating. A style less routed in the pragmatism that the UK injected, despite the down-to earth-influence of the Netherlands and Nordic countries. A style heavily influenced by the more bureaucratic Franco-German more approach. Despite these flaws, the anti-greenwashing toolbox could also prompt the EU towards a leadership role, confirming the reality of the "Brussels Effect" described by Anu Bradford.[13] Such effect might however require in the context of sustainability that, beyond serendipity, the EU seized the opportunity of playing a leadership role and rose to the challenge.

This chapter will analyze how the regulatory anti-greenwashing regulatory effort represents a worthwhile beginning but remains far from maturity. In the first section, the chapter will briefly assess the ambitious proposed sustainability due diligence requirements that are currently under discussion, which would require companies to do human rights and environmental monitoring. In the second section, the chapter will examine the EU non-financial disclosure requirements. The chapter will recognize the expected discrepancy between the commandments to "monitor" and "disclose" and their likely effects. In the third section, the chapter will then assess under which conditions the EU might nevertheless find itself in a position to play a leading international role against greenwashing.

Monitor

In February 2022, the European Commission released a draft Directive on Corporate Sustainability Due Diligence ("CSDD Directive"), which requires human rights and environmental due diligence. It creates related director duties. It also requires companies to internalize the negative externalities caused to the environment and to society. If the Directive is adopted, in due time, EU Member States will have to transpose into their domestic law a due diligence duty to identify, prevent or mitigate and, finally, end "adverse impact" for the environment and human rights.

Focusing for purposes of this chapter on environment: what qualifies as "adverse impact" is defined by reference to international conventions regarding biological diversity, mercury, and hazardous waste. This has raised concerns, since the international instruments' obligations are binding on contracting states, rather than companies, and are usually expressed in general terms, often set for all sectors globally (like the emission reduction objective).[14] How are companies to determine the content of their own obligations? The "rule book"[15] of this new field of public regulation will have to expand in order to reach the level of clarity and specificity that companies and supervisors in charge of sustainability will need.

As for reporting requirements: the CSDD Directive would not create a separate requirement but would instead complement existing disclosure duties.

Disclose

While many companies have long ago started to report non-financial elements, and for larger ones have been required to do so since 2014, the European Commission noted that information that companies report is not sufficient as their "reports often omit information that investors and other stakeholders think is important".[16] The Corporate Sustainability Reporting Directive (adopted as part of the Sustainable Finance Package of 21 April 2021),[17] the Sustainable Finance Disclosure Regulation (SFDR) adopted in Spring 2019,[18] the Communication from the Commission on Reporting Climate-Related Information,[19] and soft law principles targeting green bonds specifically,[20] have together updated the 2014 requirements on non-financial information.[21] They have enlarged its scope, as will the CSDD Directive if adopted. These rules have increased transparency at almost all levels in the financial value chain: issuers, investment funds, pension funds, hedge funds, financial advisors, asset managers (all recognized as "financial market participants"[22]), and rating agencies. In addition, in order to facilitate investors' access to data, the Commission has announced in its Capital Markets Union New Action Plan[23] the establishment of a European Single Access Point[24] for financial and non-financial information publicly disclosed by companies.

The low-carbon Benchmark Regulation set out the requirements for "EU Climate Transition Benchmarks" and "EU Paris-aligned Benchmarks", while the Taxonomy Regulation announced a unified EU classification system to label economic activity as environmentally sustainable. Such systematization seems crucial. On the one hand, as labels, indices, and principles drawn up by various uncoordinated organizations multiply, they create complexity and confusion for companies and investors. On the other hand, for capital markets to operate sustainably, it is indispensable to have non-financial information that is of the same rigour and relevance as financial information and that is also subject to the same degree of auditability.[25]

In this context, standards for non-financial information for companies' environmental (as well as social and governance) performance are important. Like accounting standards, they are accepted simplified constructs to represent a company's performance. Though imperfect (and evolving) standards enable comparability (without preventing additional information to be provided) and only fulfil their role in practice if they are mandatory.

The Taxonomy Regulation[26] was designed as a classification system and metric for sustainable reporting. Through its implementing and delegated acts, it expanded into a benchmark to measure progress towards sustainability in the EU. By making clear which economic activities contribute most to meeting the EU's environmental objectives, the Regulation is expected to guide—or nudge—investors towards "green" investments (on the model of energy consumption labelling, and its colour-gradient) and also impose pressure on economic actors to "green up".

As currently developed on the basis of the Regulation, the EU Taxonomy includes six environmental objectives: climate change mitigation, climate change adaptation, sustainable use and protection of water and marine resources, transition to a circular economy, pollution prevention and control, and protection and restoration of biodiversity and ecosystems. Companies are required to make disclosure for each of the activities they engage in, which might be numerous given the detailed classifications of the Taxonomy Regulation (e.g. plastic transformation, steel transformation, electronics manufacturing). To be classified as "taxonomy aligned", an economic activity should satisfy three conditions. First, it should make a substantial contribution to one of the six environmental objectives. Second, it should do no harm to the other five objectives. Third, it should meet minimum safeguards regarding business, labour, and human rights.

Taxonomy Delegated Acts set the indicators which consist of the Technical Screening Criteria (TSC) performance thresholds[27]: they are drafted by a Technical Expert Group, now known as the Platform on Sustainable Finance. The Delegated Act supplementing Article 8[28] of the Taxonomy Regulation was published in December 2021 to specify the content, methodology, and presentation of information to be disclosed by financial and non-financial firms concerning the proportion of environmentally sustainable economic activities in their business, investments, or lending activities. In February 2022, the Commission also approved the Complementary Delegated Act[29] to incorporate Nuclear and Gas in the TSC, introducing specific disclosure requirements for companies in these sectors.

While Article 8(1) of the Taxonomy Regulation requires large firms to disclose how their activities are associated with environmentally sustainable economic activities, Article 8(2) specifies two performance indicators (KPIs) related to turnover, capital expenditure (CapEx) and operational expenditure (OpEx) that non-financial firms are required to disclose. These disclosure requirements complement the Non-Financial Reporting Directive (NFRD)[30] by providing a common reference point.

The technical work on remaining environmental objectives is ongoing in the EU Platform on Sustainable Finance.[31] These are expected to become law through respective Delegated Acts by January 2023. However, since the laws will need to be reviewed by the EU Council and the European Parliament, they are unlikely to be completed by this date.

In summary, the EU's green finance taxonomy aims to avoid greenwashing by establishing criteria for activities and financial instruments that claim to be environmentally sustainable or to contribute to a social objective. However, it appears rather bureaucratic with the requirement to fill in multiple online forms. In addition, its activity-based linear architecture does not fully ensure that the standards are developed in a rigorous manner or sheltered from political considerations. It is possible that innovation may suffer due to standards that are quite general and binary in their application: "green" or "not green".

Because economy is global, what is really needed are standards that are also global, in addition to being independent and rigorous. This is an endeavour that requires leadership from a well-placed player.

Towards international leadership?

The EU has shown an interest in building up an international forum for transitioning towards a sustainable economy. With countries[32] representing 55% of the world's greenhouse gas emissions and half of the world's population and GDP, the EU launched the International Platform on Sustainable Finance (IPSF).[33] Although the IPSF is not a standard-setting body, its work is aimed at preparing the ground for the international standard-setters to develop globally applicable sustainable finance standards.[34]

As noted in the first IPSF annual report, the absence of coherent definitions of green investments (taxonomies) at the global level, and the low degree of standardization of reporting, represent a limit to green and sustainable finance worldwide. Moreover, around the world, several countries have drawn up roadmaps for sustainable finance. Various public and private bodies have also introduced frameworks to enhance standardization. However, these uncoordinated initiatives tend to reflect local priorities and stages of market development: they cause fragmentation.

The need to overcome this situation is also recognized in the EU–US agenda for global change[35] announced a few weeks after the election of President Joe Biden. This transatlantic initiative contemplates jointly designing a global regulatory framework for sustainable finance, based on the experience of the EU taxonomy. As such, this illustrates the leading role that Europe could play as other major economies start to prioritize a coordinated response to climate change.[36]

There is obviously a risk that collective action fails and that each entity insists on imposing its own standards rather than working towards global ones. In particular, the EU may decide that because it can mandate standards, it should do so. Unless these are endorsed by market forces, such standards might trigger a mere compliance exercise, with little benefit to companies, investors, and society as a whole.

If, however, the EU recognizes that it could be at the forefront of an international effort to help global standards emerge, it will be able to foster joint work with other bodies. Such bodies include the Impact Management Project,[37] which has engaged in an effort to reconcile the various sets of existing standards[38]; the World Economic Forum International Business Council, which can harness commitment from the corporate community[39]; and the Sustainability Standards Board[40] to sit alongside the International Accounting Standards Board and engage in a similar role establishing international reporting standards.[41] Were the EU to take on the role of facilitator, it could deliver global standards for non-financial information that US and Asian companies will adopt.

The contemplated scope for the CSDD Directive includes an extraterritorial impact, as the requirements would apply not only to companies in high-impact sectors—provided they are incorporated in the EU or have a minimum turnover or number of staff in the EU—but also to their subsidiaries. In other words, any entity part of these companies' value chain and party to an established business relationship would be required to engage in the monitoring effort described earlier, wherever it is incorporated or located, public or closely held. This last point is worth noting that important challenges for sustainability lie with closely held corporations outside of the usual scope of finance.

As has been stressed:

> [B]y design the proposed [CSDD] Directive would require adaptation to EU standards across the globe from any firm that want to be part of the value chain of any large company operation in the European market (i.e., the largest trade area in the world).[42]

The modelling ambition of the EU would be more far-reaching than in the case of the General Data Protection Regulation (GDPR): while technology companies remain free to, and often do impose to customers privacy terms and conditions outside the EU that do not comply with European requirements, such choice would not be available to companies involved in value chain of EU companies under the CSDD Directive. One may wonder whether the stance is overly ambitious—especially because some of the mechanisms are novel and not tested. Establishing leadership is not an amateur game.

Key takeaways:

- The EU has implemented regulations and directives, such as the Action Plan on Financing Sustainable Growth and the Taxonomy Regulation, to promote sustainable investments and improve transparency in non-financial reporting.
- The proposed Corporate Sustainability Due Diligence Directive aims to require companies to monitor and disclose their environmental and human rights impact, contributing to the fight against greenwashing.

- The EU's green finance taxonomy establishes criteria for environmentally sustainable activities and financial instruments. However, there are concerns about its bureaucratic nature and the potential lack of innovation due to general and binary standards.
- The EU has the potential to play a leadership role in developing global sustainable finance standards. Collaboration with international bodies and initiatives could help harmonize standards and overcome fragmentation in sustainable finance efforts worldwide.

Food for thought:

- If CSR exists, then why should companies overstep the lines of ethical behaviour that they commit to?
- To what extent can we trust companies to monitor and disclose their environmental and human rights impact? How can governments (or the EU for the European Economic Area) ensure that they do?
- Think of your own company or institution. In what ways are they tempted towards greenwashing? Have any blatant greenwashing campaigns been carried out and what have the consequences been? Have people spoken up? Why—or why not?
- Europe has a leading role in sustainability-led initiatives. Why do you think such advances have occurred when in other parts of the world sustainability is lower on the agenda and progress slow?

Notes

1 For example, in May 2021, Chevron Corporation's shareholders voted to reduce emissions from the company's customers. www.bloomberg.com/news/articles/2021-05-26/chevron-investors-back-climate-proposal-in-rebuke-to-management.

2 For example, Royal Dutch Shell PLC was ordered by a Dutch court to slash its emissions faster than planned. www.bloomberg.com/news/articles/2021-05-26/shell-loses-climate-case-that-may-set-precedent-for-oil-industry#xj4y7vzkg. A year later, the environmental group ClientEarth initiated a legal action against Shell's board members for failure to act in the preparation of energy transition. See www.clientearth.org/latest/latest-updates/news/we-re-taking-legal-action-against-shell-s-board-for-mismanaging-climate-risk/.

3 See, for example, Shell Sustainability Report (2020, p. 84): "divestments are a key part of our efforts to refresh and upgrade our portfolio as we drive towards our target to become a net-zero emissions energy business by 2050".

4 See www.nytimes.com/2022/05/10/climate/oilfield-sales-pollution.html.

5 See Armour, J., Enriques, L., & Wetzer, T. *Dark and dirty assets: Greening climate-driven asset partitioning*. www.law.ox.ac.uk/business-law-blog/blog/2022/06/dark-and-dirty-assets-greening-climate-driven-asset-partitioning.

6 https://ec.europa.eu/info/strategy/priorities-2019-2024/european-green-deal_en.

7 https://eur-lex.europa.eu/legal-content/EN/TXT/?qid=1588581905912&uri=CELEX:52020PC0080.

8 https://eur-lex.europa.eu/legal-content/EN/TXT/?uri=CELEX:52018DC0097.

9 Regulation (EU) 2019/2088 of 27 November 2019 on sustainability-related disclosures in the financial services sector that entered into force on March 10, 2021.

10 Regulation (EU) 2019/2089 of 27 November 2019 amending Regulation (EU) 2016/1011 as regards EU Climate Transition Benchmarks, EU Paris-aligned Benchmarks and sustainability-related disclosures for benchmarks. It modified the "Benchmark" Regulation (EU) 2016/1011 of the European Parliament and of the Council of 8 June 2016 on indices used as benchmarks in financial instruments and financial contracts or to measure the performance of investment funds, applicable since January 2018.
11 Regulation (EU) 2020/852.
12 https://ec.europa.eu/info/publications/proposal-directive-corporate-sustainable-due-diligence-and-annex_en.
13 Bradford, A. (2020). *The Brussels effect: How the European Union rules the world*. Oxford University Press.
14 See Ferrarini, G. (2022, April 22). Corporate sustainability due diligence and the shifting balance between soft law and hard law in the EU. *Oxford Business Law Blog*. www.law.ox.ac.uk/business-law-blog/blog/2022/04/corporate-sustainability-due-diligence-and-shifting-balance-between.
15 The analogy with the banking rule book and how it has developed might be a useful comparison. See Ferrarini n(14).
16 See Q&AQ on Corporate Sustainability Reporting Directive Proposal. https://ec.europa.eu/commission/presscorner/detail/en/qanda_21_1806.
17 It requires all large companies to publish regular reports on their environmental and social impact activities as from January 2024 for the 2023 financial year. The directive extends the scope and reporting requirements of the already-existing Non-Financial Reporting Directive which mandates large public interest entities to report on their sustainability performance since 2018.
18 It imposes disclosures to financial market participants since 10 March 2021. It enacts sustainability disclosure obligations for manufacturers of financial products and financial advisers toward end-investors; this in relation to the integration of sustainability risks by financial market participants (i.e. asset managers, institutional investors, insurance companies, pension funds, all entities offering financial products where they manage clients' money) and financial advisers in all investment processes and for financial products that pursue the objective of sustainable investment.
19 2019/C 209/01.
20 For example, sustainability bonds guidelines, updated in June 2021: http://dev.icmagroup.org/green-social-and-sustainability-bonds/sustainability-bond-guidelines-sbg/.
21 Directive 2014/95/EU of the European Parliament and of the Council of 22 October 2014 amending Directive 2013/34/EU as regards disclosure of non-financial and diversity information by certain large undertakings and groups. See https://eur-lex.europa.eu/legal-content/EN/TXT/?uri=CELEX%3A32014L0095.
22 Regulation (EU) 2019/2088 Article 2.
23 https://ec.europa.eu/info/business-economy-euro/growth-and-investment/capital-markets-union/capital-markets-union-2020-action-plan_en.
24 https://ec.europa.eu/info/consultations/finance-2021-european-single-access-point_en.
25 Eccles, R. *Here is how to set global standards for nonfinancial information*. www.accountancyeurope.eu/wp-content/uploads/Prof-Eccles_Here-Is-How-To-Set-Global-Standards-For-Nonfinancial-Information_Forbes_March_2020.pdf.
26 Regulation (EU) 2020/852 of the European Parliament and of the Council of 18 June 2020 on the establishment of a framework to facilitate sustainable investment, and amending Regulation (EU) 2019/2088.
27 The Climate Delegated Act came into force in December 2021, see https://ec.europa.eu/info/publications/210421-sustainable-finance-communication_en#taxonomy.

28 https://eur-lex.europa.eu/legal-content/EN/TXT/?uri=uriserv:OJ.L_.2021.443.01.0009.01.ENG.
29 https://ec.europa.eu/info/publications/220202-sustainable-finance-taxonomy-complementary-climate-delegated-act_en.
30 www.europarl.europa.eu/RegData/etudes/BRIE/2021/654213/EPRS_BRI(2021)654213_EN.pdf.
31 https://ec.europa.eu/info/business-economy-euro/banking-and-finance/sustainable-finance/overview-sustainable-finance/platform-sustainable-finance_en.
32 Argentina, Canada, Chile, China, India, Indonesia, Japan, Kenya, Morocco, New Zealand, Norway, Senegal, Singapore, and Switzerland.
33 https://ec.europa.eu/info/business-economy-euro/banking-and-finance/sustainable-finance/international-platform-sustainable-finance_en.
34 See IPSF annual report October 2020: https://ec.europa.eu/info/sites/default/files/business_economy_euro/banking_and_finance/documents/international-platform-sustainable-finance-annual-report-2020_en.pdf.
35 https://eur-lex.europa.eu/legal-content/EN/TXT/?uri=JOIN:2020:22:FIN.
36 For the US approach, see Ho, Virginia H. (2022) *Modernizing ESG disclosure.* University of Illinois Law Review, p. 277 https://illinoislawrev.web.illinois.edu/wp-content/uploads/2022/01/Harper-Ho.pdf.
37 https://impactmanagementproject.com.
38 The IMP facilitates a network of practitioners aiming at sharing and harmonizing their expertise in non-financial reporting and impact measurement for the benefit of companies and investors.
39 Recently, 140 CEOs gave support to 22 metrics to be reported on www.weforum.org/whitepapers/toward-common-metrics-and-consistent-reporting-of-sustainable-value-creation.
40 It was established in September 2020. www.ifrs.org/news-and-events/news/2020/09/ifrs-foundation-trustees-consult-on-global-approach-to-sustainability-reporting/.
41 International Financial Reporting Standards (IFRS) are used by all major countries in the world, except the United States, which uses US Generally Accepted Accounting Principles established by the Financial Accounting Standards Board.
42 Enriques, L., & Gatti, M. (2022, April 21). The extra-territorial impact of the proposed EU Directive on corporate sustainability due diligence: Why corporate America should pay attention. *Oxford Business Law Blog*. www.law.ox.ac.uk/business-law-blog/blog/2022/04/extraterritorial-impact-proposed-eu-directive-corporate.

Part III

From products and profit to responsible innovation

7 Responsible innovation as a driving force for ecological transition

Xavier Pavie

How far should we take innovation?

As a result of innovation, animal populations and species are disappearing. The massive development of technologies, products, consumer and non-consumer goods has had—and continues to have—a direct consequence on the depletion of natural resources. Moreover, given a growing body of scientific evidence, it is now undisputable that the atmosphere, soil and oceans are deteriorating due to anthropogenic activity and our constant quest for economic growth. Increasing urbanisation too is profoundly and lastingly changing the balance of the biosphere.

Indeed, these challenges are global: acid rain and radioactive pollution know no borders, and the "7th continent" made of plastic is adrift in the Pacific beyond national waters. In sum, these are the direct consequence of the unpredictability of the innovations introduced onto a market, a telling example being that of chlorofluorocarbons (CFCs). Launched in the 1950s, there was no way of knowing that in the 1970s and 1980s we would discover that they were dangerous greenhouse gases and were causing stratospheric ozone depletion.

In the 16th century, French philosopher François Rabelais said "*Knowledge without conscience is but the ruin of the soul*",[1] proving himself to be particularly visionary. This observation does not apply only to the environmental impact of science: electronics have invaded our everyday lives with communicating objects. As such, the "digitalisation of the world" is becoming a global challenge, and nanotechnologies are ubiquitous in food, clothing, furniture, cars, to name but a few. And this is certainly only the beginning, considering the advances still to come in the exploitation of the human body and its avatars with the trivialisation of automation.

At the same time, emerging digital technologies, alongside new means of communication which derive from them, have been instrumental in democratic upheavals, enabling populations to raise international awareness about complex political situations, and in circumventing limitations to freedom of expression in order to rally public opinion to their cause. On the other hand, medical advances, supported by technology, are praised by their beneficiaries.

DOI: 10.4324/9781003522355-10

In light of this, the concept of innovation, like that of science, should be put into perspective with the Greek term *deinon*, which expresses both what is terrific and terrifying—concepts which merge together to express the power of opposites. Sophocles illustrated this idea in *Antigone* with the example of man: "*Skilful beyond hope is the contrivance of his art and he advances sometimes to evil at other times to good*".[2] Indeed, it is the man, the individual, who proposes an innovation, and who—whether consciously or unconsciously—can make an innovation lean towards evil or towards good.

There was a period when religion weighed so heavily on the collective consciousness and institutions that it inhibited certain possibilities for progress—for example, in reproductive choices. Today, this constraint has completely disappeared, at least from the lab benches. Moreover, scientists have not always had the means to fulfil their ambitions. In the last few decades, however, there has been a clear technical and technological acceleration with the increase in genetic knowledge, our growing understanding of DNA structures and the advent of cloning. Today, the problem is no longer an issue of moral acceptance or scientific capability. It is an issue of duty to do or not to do in the name of ethics and responsibility.[3]

Progress can be seen as a meta-model for change, dealing with the general perspective of evolution, that of knowledge, with hope for the future of mankind. Innovation, on the other hand, refers to more precise, technically, scientifically and socially targeted developments, often considered in relation to the market. In a way, then, innovation is the child of progress, constantly seeking to adapt to the needs of individuals. Moreover, innovation has enabled the emergence of products and services which less than a century ago were considered pure science fiction. This is the case of transhumanism, whose self-professed aim is to improve the human condition through life-enhancing techniques, such as eliminating ageing and increasing intellectual, physical or psychological capacities.[4]

Transition through responsible innovation: being accountable for one's actions

To a certain extent, the term "responsible" is polysemic—it can have multiple meanings to different people—and maybe even trivialised. What does responsibility mean today? For whom? To what extent? Within what limits? What does it mean to be responsible in an unprecedented context of increasing technology and its escalating impacts, and at a time when globalisation is accelerating? From here onwards, the human being is forced to assume responsibility *for* the world and *in* the world. More particularly, the Innovator is concerned with the responsibility of the world they design through the new products and services they launch on the market.

The responsibility of the Innovator is all the more important as they find themselves in a new context which articulates both the modern period in which we live, and the search for sustainable and responsible development with a view to preserving mankind and its environment. Thanks to advances in science and technology, we now have an understanding of the world in all its complexities and in how we exploit it. These developments offer a plethora of possible actions, but at the same time raise ethical, social and civic questions given the new risks generated by these developments. Moreover, it is impossible to determine these ahead of time, whether in terms of success or unforeseen applications. French author François Ost explains that in this context, responsibility needs to be redistributed, for we

> now appear responsible, or at least co- responsible, for a collective action whose developments and effects are largely unknown to us, and so, the circle of proximity which made me accountable only towards those close to me and my neighbours is broken, and so, the bond of simultaneity which made me accountable for the immediate, or at least proximate, effects of the actions I take today is distorted.[5]

The frameworks of responsibility and caution are evolving because so too is the breadth of our ability to act, even compared to 30 years ago. Responsibility remains individual, but extends globally. It is attributable to a subject, but not only.

Moreover, whereas responsibility was formerly linked to proximity, to a clear spatio-temporal delimitation, it has now become timeless, spatially boundless and with unlimited multi- reciprocity. In other words, responsibility needs to be reconsidered because the back and forth between individual and global responsibility is as confusing as it is intense. Jean-Louis Genard explains:

> More than clearly identifiable actions, we are faced with a multiplicity of decisions which, together, can have far-reaching effects. In short, responsibility is both everywhere and nowhere. Actions have been taken, decisions have been made, sometimes with dramatic consequences. But responsibilities are not identifiable at all, unless they relate to the organisation or the network, which does not correspond to our spontaneous understanding of the idea of responsibility. The latter remains attached to individualised identification.[6]

To this, we might add that it has the effect of diluting responsibility.

Although the very concept of responsibility can be difficult to grasp spontaneously (as it is often associated with ethical, moral, respect and awareness issues), it has a very precise definition, on which its Latin etymology sheds light: *respondere*, that is, to answer for one's actions. This makes sense with liability as defined in the French Civil Code: "*Any act whatever of man, which causes damage to another, obliges the one by whose fault it occurred, to compensate it*".[7] To answer for one's actions is to take responsibility for them, to recognise oneself as the perpetrator. Furthermore, responsibility also has a moral dimension. It refers to the moral obligation to right a wrong, to fulfil a duty, to assume the consequences of one's acts.

There is also a link between responsibility and freedom. To be free is to take responsibility for one's actions. To be responsible is to be able to answer for them, precisely because of this freedom. Consequently, a prudent man who wants to be absolutely free will take on as few responsibilities as possible, simply because it will be difficult for him to assume them. If we can be free, independent in society, what about when we are at work? Can we, as managers, preserve the freedom we cherish as citizens? The hierarchical structures, and the administrative and operational organisation of companies are difficult to reconcile with freedom. However, individuals can only be held accountable for their own actions if they are completely free. In an economic context, where the labour market is in a constant state of tension between supply and demand, employees do not feel totally free to accept or refuse certain demands from their management.

The versatile nature of the concept of "responsibility" is also reflected in language. In English, there are three different words to define the notion of responsibility: *responsibility*, *liability* and *accountability*.[8] The latter term very directly implies the notion of being accountable to others: to a board of directors, to the general public, to customers. Innovation must be thought out in the light of these new constraints and the multiplicity of responsibilities which are emerging. Since responsibility has different connotations and meanings, it cannot be understood in the same way by all players in a globalised economy. This necessarily leads to misunderstandings about what to do from one country to another, and from one culture to another.

Without even questioning the problems of language, the notion of responsibility is, by nature, complex—not only because it involves others but also because it expresses several dimensions within the same individual. At the same time, we are manager, innovator, citizen, parent, husband and wife. This raises the very clear issue of the interaction between the private and professional spheres, and the interdependence between managers and citizens, between innovators and the recipients of the innovation as a whole. Is the action I am taking as a manager one I would wish for as a citizen? As Marc Neuberg sums up, the responsibility of innovation lies in the consideration of situation within a value system shared by all the actors impacted by that process.[9]

Towards the principle of responsible innovation

We cannot date the emergence of the concept of responsible innovation. It is the result of a set of catalysts, a chronological process integral to the issue of corporate social responsibility, which originally came about as a way of examining the involvement of the business world in in society. Howard Bowen, considered the founding father of corporate social responsibility, is one such example. He defines the social responsibility of managers as "*the obligations of businessmen to pursue those policies, to make those decisions, or to follow those lines of action that are desirable in terms of the objectives and values of our society*".[10] However, the issues of corporate social responsibility have little practical relevance to innovation.

More recently, Gro Harlem Brundtland, in her 1987 report on the concept of sustainable development,[11] shows how important it is to take future generations into account in our actions within organisations. More precisely, to succeed in defining viable schemes which reconcile the three ecological, social and economic aspects of human activities: the "three pillars" to be taken into account by communities, businesses and individuals.

As for responsible innovation itself, it can be traced back to philosopher Hans Jonas. In *The Imperative of Responsibility* Jonah questions whether humanity should continue to exist.[12] If the answer is yes, then humanity must adopt a new behaviour of care and concern for the world. This duty of care is incumbent upon the Innovator, since they are the pillar of responsibility towards civil society. This is both worrying and encouraging because it implies that if the Innovator does indeed have such a hold on society by deploying new ideas, new products and innovations, then, by corollary, they can also change the world by integrating the dimension of responsibility into their projects. This is the principle of responsible innovation. In 1979, in *The Imperative of Responsibility*, Jonas had already developed the idea that human knowledge surpasses predictive knowledge, without employing the actual label of responsible innovation. It is therefore fundamental, in his view, to develop an ethical approach so as to close this gap. Without rejecting science and technology, Jonas exposes the need to deploy a humane form of responsibility so as to face up to the risks inherently brought on by technology and which imperil humanity.

The strength of responsible innovation: three pillars for an effective transition

Extensive research has been carried out in order to define responsible innovation, under the initial impetus of Bernadette Bensaude-Vincent.[13] More specifically, three interacting determinants have been developed for understanding the challenges of responsible innovation. These determinants can interact but must also be considered separately from one other.

Questioning the answers to be given to the needs of individuals

This first pillar of responsible innovation is decisive: must we always respond to the needs of individuals? We have already addressed the issue of needs and more specifically that we do not create needs but rather respond to conscious or unconscious latent needs. That being said, is it because a need exists that we must necessarily meet it?

Responsible innovation questions the obsession of organisations of having to systematically respond to the needs of individuals by challenging the relevance of the systematic provision of a response to every single need detected. Indeed, should a company systematically launch the innovation which meets an identified need? In other words, just because there is a need does not necessarily mean that there has to be an answer. Should innovation strategies systematically have the reflex of setting innovation in motion as soon as a need is detected? For example, is it because high school students do not want to do their homework that we need to launch an online service where others do their homework for them?[14] Or is it because a fraction of the population has certain sexual desires that we need to organise holidays which meet this demand?[15] If consumers want to listen to music while on the go, outside of their car and their living room, while commuting, on a walk or running, and with great practicality thanks to dematerialisation, is it, however, necessary and justified to have 20 different generations of iPods in less than ten years, when we know that the construction of each device requires the extraction of rare earth elements, a process known to be particularly polluting? Is it because individuals want to become homeowners that we should necessarily develop services at all costs to enable them to purchase their dream house for which they do not really have the debt capacity?

Measuring the direct consequences of innovations

This dimension is linked to two elements: on the one hand, the uncertainty of implementing any innovation and, on the other hand, the inability to anticipate the impacts of products or services on the health of current users and their lifestyles, as well as on future customers.

This inability to predict is all the more acute because, at the same time, there is an innovation race which leads to rapid, sometimes even hasty decisions. The competitive environment and the atomisation of markets compel competitors to launch their latest innovation as quickly as possible, without really considering the consequences. As an example, we might mention the tragic and infamous case of the Ford Pinto, a car which was left on the market even when it was known that there was a risk of the petrol tank exploding at the slightest shock.[16] In this example, this was due to the blatant dishonesty of the company's leader; other times, however, business leaders might do the right thing to avoid any risk. For example, the exact impact of radiation from mobile phones to the heart or other organs remains unclear—the scientific studies carried out on the subject are still far from conclusive and are often divergent. This is a direct consequence of the innovation, and the Innovator must understand that they bear responsibility for what they are potentially doing to the recipient of the innovation. In the case of subprime mortgages, the direct impact was obvious, and the innovator ought to have put in place a system for protecting those who were going to benefit from this scheme (or maybe even turn them down when this was relevant). We can also consider the example of consumer credit. On a regular basis, commercial courts recall the catastrophic situations of families facing over-indebtedness. The spiral in which these households find themselves is very often the result of revolving loans, taken out through major retailers, but also through the websites of specialised credit institutions when they make a purchase or when they have an exceptional need. The direct impact of this proposal is the delicate situation in which the borrower will find himself obliged to repay the credit with interest rates which can be more than excessive. Finally, let's not forget the massive appearance of robots in industry and in everyday life, which could destroy up to 70% of jobs in the coming years.[17] This is a direct consequence of innovation, and it does not necessarily mean that this innovation has to be eliminated, but simply that the consequences must be considered and the question must be asked as to whether it is possible to assist the most-affected categories of workers in this inevitable change.

Considering the indirect impacts of innovations

The third and last pillar concerns the need to consider that an innovation has consequences beyond the framework from which it emerged. In order to achieve this, we must fully accept the idea that we all interact with each other consciously or unconsciously and within an ecosystem. Whereas the previous axis concerned the impacts of innovation on its users, here it is a question of considering that the launch of an innovation will certainly have an impact on its customers, but that non-customers might also be impacted.

A certain maturity is required to achieve this degree of responsibility, since we are talking about being accountable to someone who exists outside of the scope of our actions. The innovation brought about by a scientist or a product manager can induce sectorial permeability which had not initially been foreseen. For example, this could be the launch of a new, faster, more powerful aircraft, but which presents the downside of emitting higher noise levels. The Innovator needs to assess the consequences of the innovation not only in terms of flight crew, ground staff and customers, but also in terms of the impact on local residents, whether human or animal. It is the entire ecosystem around airports which is affected, as highlighted by the *Grenelle de l'environnement* summit in France, which outlined a package of measures to be taken.[18] The same is true when selling an air-conditioned vehicle which will consume on average 15% more fuel than a car which does not use this option.[19] The CO_2 emissions will impact not only the driver of the vehicle but also passers-by and cyclists with whom the car will share the road.

A further example is the construction of dwellings near a road which has a direct consequence on the development of the lungs of those who live there, even if they themselves never use these roads. Or the nanomaterials in Japanese socks that offer great comfort and mean that socks remain odourless. However, when the socks are washed, the nanomaterials end straight up in the wastewater which can be discharged into rivers, the sea, eaten by fish, and come into contact with plants. In sum, these are the indirect impacts causing the entire ecosystem to be disrupted. The subprime crisis, for instance, did not only affect customers and lenders but also those who were totally unrelated to this proposal but who, through the financial game of securitisation, were negatively impacted by this innovation. When we put our savings in a savings account or a life insurance policy, for example, what is this money used for? Do banks invest these funds in companies which may indirectly harm citizens?

These three questions are fundamental in initiating a responsible innovation process. Faced with the impossibility of controlling the uncertainty of innovation, these considerations are intended to help the players of innovation to at least measure it.

Responsible innovation as a tool for transition

In the ten or so years since the emergence of the idea of responsible innovation, a number of organisations have begun to take a close interest in this concept, whether in the energy, communication[20] or automotive sectors. Following the financial crisis of 2007, banks and insurance companies had no choice but to rethink their innovation process.[21]

Responsible innovation seems a useful tool to help the transition—from a traditional way to innovate to a responsible one which would take into account environmental, political as well as human issues. As a result of innovation, we have harmed the planet, our ecosystem. There is no choice but to repair it, take care of it, help the planet recover and heal the causes—we need to rethink innovation through responsibility.

Key takeaways:

- Progress can be seen as a meta-model for change, dealing with the general perspective of evolution, that of knowledge, with hope for the future of humankind. Innovation refers to more precise, technically, scientifically and socially targeted developments, often considered in relation to the market.
- Given the climate crisis, the human being is forced to assume responsibility *for* the world and *in* the world. The Innovator is concerned with the responsibility of the world they design through the new products and services they launch on the market.
- Responsibility finds its root in the Latin word *respondere*—to answer for one's actions. To answer for one's actions is to take responsibility for them, to recognise oneself as the perpetrator. Responsibility also has a moral dimension. It refers to the moral obligation to right a wrong, to fulfil a duty, to assume the consequences of one's acts.
- In English, there are three different words to define the notion of responsibility: *responsibility*, *liability* and *accountability*.
- This first pillar of responsible innovation is decisive: must we always respond to the needs of individuals?

- The second pillar: Measuring the direct consequences of innovations: the uncertainty of implementing any innovation and the inability to anticipate the impacts of products or services on the health of current users and their lifestyles, as well as on future customers.
- The third pillar: Considering the indirect impacts of innovations: an innovation has consequences beyond the framework from which it emerged. Whereas the previous axis concerned the impacts of innovation on its users, here it is a question of considering that the launch of an innovation will certainly have an impact on its customers, but that non-customers might also be impacted.
- Responsible innovation is a useful tool to help the transition—from a traditional way to innovate to a responsible one that takes into account environmental, political as well as human issues.

Food for thought:

- Look back at previous decades. Which innovations from the 1950s to the 1970s positively changed the world for the consumer? To what extent did they harm the planet? How have they changed since to take on the dimension of respect for the environment?
- Which brands in modern times have embodied responsible innovation? How have they done that?
- To what extent is the well-being of the planet and society the responsibility of the consumer—and not the innovator's? And how do both demonstrate disrespect or respect for the environment and society?

Notes

1 Rabelais, F. *Gargantua and Pantagruel, complete. Five books of the lives, heroic deeds and sayings of Gargantua and his son Pantagruel.* Translated into English by Sir Thomas Urquhart of Cromarty and Peter Antony Motteux. www.gutenberg.org/files/1200/1200-h/1200-h.htm.
2 Sophocle, *Antigone*, trad. P. Mazon, Les Belles Lettres, 1955, p. 86. Sophocle, *Antigone*, Loeb Classical Library. Translated to English by Hugh Lloyd-Jones.
3 The birth of the first "saviour sibling" in France 2012 is one of many examples. The parents of a little girl with a genetic disease decided to have a second child in order to save their first born. The parents of this "saviour sibling" benefited from a double preimplantation genetic diagnosis. The embryos carrying the disease were discarded, and the medical team selected from among the healthy embryos the one most compatible with the genetic makeup of the first born and implanted it in the mother's womb. This is a formidable technical prowess, but one cannot help but wonder about the development of such a success which borders on eugenics.
4 www.transhumanism.org.
5 Ost, F. La Nature hors la loi. *La Découverte*, p. 267. Our translation.
6 Genard, J.-L. (2000). Le temps de la responsabilité. In G. Philippe, O. François, & V. K. Michel (Eds.), *L'Accélération du temps juridique* (pp. 105–125). Publications des Facultés universitaires, Saint-Louis. Our translation.
7 Article 1240 of the French Civil Code (version of 2016). Translated to English by John Cartwright, Bénédicte Fauvarque-Cosson and Simon Whittaker.

8 Responsibility concerns the responsibilities incumbent upon a person, the things they are in charge of, and liability essentially concerns legal issues, while accountability refers to questions of transparency, towards the population for example.

9 *La Responsabilité: questions philosophiques* de Marc Neuberg. Presses universitaires de France, 1997.

10 Bowen, H. (1953). *Social responsibilities of the businessman* (p. 236). Harper & Brothers.

11 Brundtland, G. H. (1987). *Our common future—Report of the World Commission on Environment and Development.* United Nations General Assembly.

12 Jonas, H. (1985). *The imperative of responsibility: In search of an ethics for the technological age.* University of Chicago Press.

13 See the editorial by Bernadette Bensaude-Vincent, at the *Colloque innovation responsable* of April 29, 2009, Collège de France. (2013). *Responsible innovation: Managing the responsible emergence of science and innovation in society* (R. Owen, J. Bessant, & M. Heintz, Eds.). Wiley. *Introduction to responsible innovation criteria: A guide to entrepreneurs and innovation*, Interreg IV B-207G—KARIM Project is co-financed by the European Union. Pavie, X., Scholten, V., & Carthy, D. (2014). *Responsible innovation, from concept to practice.* World Scientific.

14 *Libération*, March 7, 2009, "Faismesdevoirs.com ferme déjà ses pages."

15 Examples of websites include pleasuretours.com; alternativephuket.com; globalfantasies.com; temptation.originalresorts.com; affordable-adult-vacations.com; wildwomenvacations.com; pornweek.com.

16 Raymond, J. (2003, March). La Ford Pinto: le contre-exemple américain. *Le Polyscope Le journal de l'École polytechnique de Montréal, 36.*

17 Arntz, M., Gregory, T., & Zierahn, U. (2016). *The risk of automation for jobs in OECD countries: A comparative analysis* (OECD Social, Employment and Migration Working Papers, No. 189). OECD Publishing. http://dx.doi.org/10.1787/5jlz9h56dvq7-en

18 www.vie-publique.fr/eclairage/268585-le-grenelle-de-lenvironnement-quels-engagements. It should also be noted that measures to reduce noise pollution for the well-being of local residents also increase aircraft kerosene consumption at the same time.

19 Gagnepain, L. (2006). La climatisation automobile, impacts, consommation et pollution. In *Repères*. French Environment and Energy Management Agency—Transport Technologies Department.

20 As an example, the Engie group and La Poste in the Lorraine region developed a number of relatively structured think tank on responsible innovation, particularly between 2010 and 2015.

21 In France, the "Club Innovation Finance" has been running a project called DRiM for almost two years to help its members develop a responsible innovation process based on Design Thinking techniques. See Pavie, X., Jouanny, C., Carthy, D., & Verez, F. (2014). *Le design thinking au service de l'innovation responsable.* Maxima.

8 Replacing old with new

Perceived product obsolescence—its impact on consumer behaviour and the planet

Emmanuelle Le Nagard

Extending the service life of electric and electronic goods is a major ecological issue. Their anticipated renewal—or replacement purchase—cause a large increase in waste and the production of new goods which generates additional CO_2 emissions that could have been avoided. The figures speak for themselves. According to ADEME, the French Agency for Ecological Transition, if every French household extended the service life of their goods by one year, approximately 6 million tonnes of CO_2 emissions could be saved over a period of ten years—that is, 0.6 million tonnes per year.

The service life of hard goods varies from one category of goods to another. According to their indicators on after sales service, French electrical retail group FNAC-Darty estimates that a French consumer keeps her smartphone for a period of 18 months, whereas she renews her TV set every seven to eight years.

The life cycle of a product—between the moment it begins functioning and the moment it is replaced—also raises a variety of business and management issues. Product life cycle is crucial for manufacturers and distributors—the shorter the service life, the more consumers are likely to replace their products and, as such, generate sales and additional profits. This ties in with a spate of criticism over recent years, with accusations that brands deliberately shorten the life span of their products to incite consumers to replace them. Indeed, this has accelerated the debate around programmed obsolescence and the "throw-away" society.

Programmed obsolescence aside, studies have described obsolescence *per se* as one of the main factors which lead consumers to replace their products. Generally defined as the decrease in the service life of a material product, this obsolescence can also be *absolute*—that is, when the product is broken or no longer works—and also *perceived*—that is, relative or partial when the replacement is linked to tech or fashion motives.

In the case of smartphones, perceived obsolescence can depend both on cognitive factors such as the introduction of new, better performing technology, and affective factors such as a nostalgic, personal relationship with the phone.

DOI: 10.4324/9781003522355-11

Indeed, most research has focused on the mobile phone, a unique object in that it offers strong social, affective, safety, and tech aspects all in one.

But focusing only on the mobile phone limits the capacity to apply the results obtained from research across product families and consumers as a whole. What about the perception of product usage value relative to different categories of products? And in which way does this perceived obsolescence explain the decision to replace hard goods that still function?

With this in mind, and with fellow researchers Valérie Guillard and Gisele de Campos Ribeiro, I set out to understand in a comprehensive way the factors of perceived obsolescence according to different product categories. First is by surveying a panel of consumers and then identifying the impact of perceived obsolescence on the decision to replace, or not, a product. In doing so, we reveal several ways in which both brands and consumers can promote awareness, thereby contributing to the now urgent need to contribute to sustainable practices in light of the climate crisis.

The various facets of perceived obsolescence

Several studies have highlighted the fact that the user value of a hard good tends to decrease over time due to the increase in costs for the owner. These costs can relate to maintenance and repairs, higher consumption of energy as the product ages, or the purchase, sometimes quasi-mandatory, of peripheral products such as adapters, special earphones, or other such accessories. The value to the owner can also decrease in terms of perceived product benefits—for example, wear and tear, or boredom or weariness with the product. To return to mobile phones, it has been shown that the owner's decision to replace this product occurs at the moment where the perceived usage value drops to almost zero.

As such, marketing defines perceived obsolescence as the relative loss of value of an object. This loss in value can be due to a change in design and style, or the improvement in the quality of products recently released on the market.

Going back to the 1960s, three dimensions of obsolescence were identified. The first of these, *obsolescence of function*, is linked to the notion that a new product launched on the market fulfils the function of the existing product in a better way. The second, *obsolescence of quality*, relates to product wear and tear. And finally, *obsolescence of desirability* refers to the design and aesthetic appeal of the owned product appearing less desirable. More recent research has also pointed to the identification of three dimensions of partial or relative obsolescence: technological, economic, and psychological.

Here, *technological obsolescence* concerns products which are substituted by another which has better performance, perceived as having better technology and new functionalities, and which fulfil the expected function in a better way. *Economic obsolescence* occurs when consumers decide to renew their product because the cost of using it, or the cost of maintenance of the current produce is much higher than that of a new product. This can also be due to the fact that the perceived cost, as well as the real cost of purchasing a new model, is less than the cost of repairing the old one. The roots of *psychological obsolescence* are to be found in the change in perception of fashion, the aesthetic quality, or even the social status attached to an existing product—in sum, the product no longer corresponds to the perception that the consumer has of herself. Lastly, *social obsolescence* is associated with peer pressure—how friends and family see the product we own.

How does perceived obsolescence affect the replacement of products? and what happens to them?

Studies relating to replacement purchases have essentially had an economic approach to predict the moment consumers replace their cars, computers, and TV sets. It's important here to mention two types of different consumer: those who *often* replace their products—generally by attraction to novelty—and those who *rarely* replace their goods, only doing so when the product breaks down, becomes dangerous to use, or has faulty functioning.

Several factors influence—positively or negatively—the frequency by which consumers replace their goods. These include situational factors such as the promotional launch of a new product, a change in family composition, a change in revenue, or a modification of the conditions of use of a product. Moreover, personal factors can also influence consumers' decisions to replace goods—age or level of education, for example—or personality factors such as an attraction to novelty, or even a tendency to keep everything.

Other studies have focused on the emotions that a decision to replace a good engenders and notably the mixed and contradictory feelings we may have when separating ourselves from something. These emotions may include doubt, sadness, nostalgia, dread, and annoyance. And this is particularly true when the product is still usable and hasn't been swapped at a vendor's. As such, the process of purchasing a new product is inseparable from that regarding the fate reserved to the product which is to be replaced. Okada's research in 2001 explains further: the decision to replace a product comes at a time when consumers can benefit or make someone else benefit from the residual value of an object. In essence, the consumer will weigh up two costs: economic—in the sense of a gain/loss of money linked to the replacement—and psychological—the cost of throwing the object on the scrapheap and the benefits of giving it away or upcycling or recycling it.

Indeed, the consumer may adopt various ways to deal with the object she wants to replace: selling it, giving it away to close ones or a charity, keeping it in the drawer or attic, or leaving it on the pavement, to name a few. All in all, this leads us to think that the decision to replace a product notably depends on the perceived obsolescence of a product.

A path towards conscious consumerism: inform, inform, and inform

A basis for our research centred on a series of interviews on the theme of product obsolescence with a panel of consumers aged 28–65. We discovered five dimensions thanks to the interviews and questionnaires: social, technological, ecological, commercial, design. A further study among 150 young consumers enabled us to develop a measurement scale that enabled us to demonstrate that perceived product obsolescence indeed has an influence on the intention to replace—indeed rapidly—products and how these consumers get rid of them.

From a societal point of view, several recommendations can be drawn up. On the one hand, in so far as the effect of perceived obsolescence on the decision to replace a product is important when taking into consideration the negative impact on the environment, it is essential to limit this practice. Moreover, it notably depends on the frequency that manufacturers launch new versions. These new versions may bring new functionalities or added value to usage. Others may be false innovations, but which contribute to giving the consumer the impression that current products are out of fashion. Improved comparative product information—drafted either by the distributors or by consumer associations—could indeed provide customers with a truer vision of the real value in the innovation and limit premature replacements.

On the other hand, highlighting the value of two new dimensions to obsolescence—the ecological and re-sale value—opens up avenues to explore reducing this perceived obsolescence, once again by better informing customers.

Concerning re-sale, a contradictory effect might be triggered on a circular economy dimension. This is because by showing the re-sale price of old models on the second-hand market, it may become less expensive for the customer to re-sell in order to buy a more recent model. In this light, limiting the price tag for exchange of products could actually slow down or prevent this effect.

The ecological dimension leads to a paradox: consumers with an affirmed sustainability conscience may be led to renew their equipment to adopt one with improved environmental performance—without taking into account the environmental cost of production of the new product, nor the potential cost of treating the waste generated by the old product. Improved information and communication will also enable consumers to make a more enlightened choice.

All in all, we—as consumers—must bear in mind our part and our role in the ecological transition and the fight against climate crisis. Our part necessarily calls for consciousness and courage—we have indeed contributed to the humankind's negative effect on the planet and the acceleration of climate change. Our part also calls for awareness of the effect of our purchasing behaviours. And this must be supported by responsibility from the manufacturers who put their products on the shelves—and a good dose of transparency through informing their customers on the impact of their products on the environment. And finally, our role as enlightened consumers is to stop and consider—and to reconsider the veracity of the perceived obsolescence we have of the objects we own.

Key takeaways:

- Perceived obsolescence, influenced by factors such as technological advancements and social comparison, significantly impacts consumers' inclination to replace durable goods that are still functioning.
- Their anticipated renewal—or replacement purchase—both cause a large increase in waste and the production of new goods which generates additional CO^2 emissions that could have been avoided.
- Psychological factors, such as dissatisfaction with the current durable goods and the desire for novelty and variety, contribute to the intention to replace even a functioning product.
- Understanding the intricate dynamics between perceived obsolescence and consumer decision-making can help marketers and policymakers develop strategies to address consumer behaviour and promote sustainable consumption.
- Improved comparative product information from manufacturers, distributors or consumer associations could provide customers with a truer vision of the real value in the innovation and limit premature replacements.
- Limiting the price tag for exchange of products could slow down or prevent the effect of consumers seeing it as advantageous to re-sell their products to purchase new ones.
- Improved information and communication can enable consumers to make a more enlightened choice, especially on the environmental cost of production of a new product or the potential cost of treating waste generated by their old product.

Food for thought:

- Think about your own situation. Which electronic or other product have you recently replaced by a new one? What made you come to the decision to discard your old device? To what extent was this decision linked to the various factors in this chapter?
- Pick three object—goods—that you own. Which brand incites you to add to your purchase by including necessary accessories in its range of peripheral products? Which brand provided you, as a consumer, with information on its environmental impact? Which brand brings out one or more new and enhanced variants in a year?
- Which brand would you consider most responsible among the three? Why?
- If the aim of a manufacturer or brand is to earn profit, how can they be encouraged to develop sustainable business models that ensure this while simultaneously bringing benefit to the planet?

Related research

Guillard, V., Le Nagard, E., & de Campos Ribeiro, G. (2023). A typology of consumers regarding perceived obsolescence: The paradox of eco-conscious consumers. *Journal of Cleaner Production*, *412*, 137202.

References

Mani, Z. (2015). *L'obsolescence programmée: quand le consommateur imagine le "prêt à jeter"* (Working Paper). https://hal.archives-ouvertes.fr/hal-01104669/document

Okada, E. M. (2001). Trade-ins, mental accounting, and product replacement decisions. *Journal of Consumer Research*, *27*(4), 433–446.

Part IV

Sustainability

The role of education and engagement

9 A pragmatic way to teach energy transition stakes in a business school

Laurence de Carlo

If she wants to teach ecological transition in higher education, a professor reads that programmes should encompass the subject's complexity through interdisciplinarity. And that teaching ecological transition means redesigning the entire range of programmes and courses of all schools and universities (collectif FORTES, 2020; Jouzel, 2022; Von der Leyen, 2022).

Such a change has become a subject of reflection in numerous institutions nowadays (de Carlo, 2020), including ESSEC Business School, with a campus presence in France, Singapore and Morocco. The magnitude and the multi-level difficulties of the task mean that it takes time. Without waiting for large-scale changes to occur, what can a Paris-based professor do at her level?

Indeed, she can define a base of knowledge and skills relevant for the course she wants to create or modify. Official documents require the building of common knowledge bases as the main tool for teaching students ecological transition (Jouzel, 2022; Von der Leyen, 2022). At the end of 2022, a professor in a business school could count on the base of knowledge and skills in ecological matters for business students developed by the French NGO *The Shift Project* and its partners (The Shift Project, 2022). This very useful definition of relevant knowledge and skills can have several pedagogical statutes. Should it be used as the only base for a course—that is, used in order to build a course only conceived as the transmission of knowledge and skills by the professor through various methods and hoped to be known, integrated and appropriated by the students at the end?

The base of a course on ecological matters in a business school can be of another order with, on the one hand, considering the knowledge and skills taught by the professor as one dimension of the course, and on the other, privileging the students' learning process in a pragmatic way (Dewey, 1916). As an example of such a pedagogical choice, let us focus on the elective course *Energy transition stakes* that I have taught in the ESSEC Master in Management programme since 2015.

DOI: 10.4324/9781003522355-13

The course's history

In 2009, I first created an elective course on *Water management stakes* in the same programme. With a maximum number of 35 authorized students and a minimum of 25 required ones, the course opened each year until 2014. The enrolled students were already sufficiently aware of the crucial dimension of water management for life on Earth, and its particular importance for the economy, to choose such an apparently bizarre course for a business school (de Carlo, 2013). Despite the critical role of water management, in 2015 I changed the course theme while keeping the same pedagogical principles: it became *Energy transition stakes*. Indeed, energy transition is not only as important as water is for life on Earth—it is also a domain in which more business students could contribute in many different companies and organizations at large. Moreover, energy transition stakes can be considered as a necessary culture for all managers and citizens, whatever their profession.

That said, there is no one best way to create a course on *Energy transition stakes* in a business school. However, this chapter will describe and analyse the example of one course by shedding light on the pedagogical choices made. First, we will describe the course context. Then, we will discuss the three main objectives of the course—that is, problematization learning process, a sharing experiment and passing on knowledge and skills.

The evolving institutional course context

First, the course content depends on several dimensions of context, in particular other related courses offered and types of students. In 2015, there was no related course at ESSEC. In 2016, my economist colleague Estefania Santacreu-Vasut created the elective course now named *Environmental economics*, and then several others saw the light of day, mainly offered within the framework of chairs created in partnership with firms: the *Ecological transition talents* chair, the *Sustainable finance* chair and the *Circular economy* chair.

At the institutional level and before 2021, students did not benefit from an introduction to climate change. As such, during the initial years, the course had to teach the fundamentals of the energy transition. Then, between 2021 and 2022, all students begin their curriculum by participating in a Climate Day initiative that includes a Climate Fresco workshop in order to sensitize them to climate stakes. Featuring very strong qualities, the Climate Fresco's main one is the opportunity to discover a phenomenon with others in a fun and engaging way that very often leads to an experience of discovery and enlightenment. Nevertheless, a significant share of students from the *Energy transition stakes* course, at least, were seen to quickly forget notions and phenomena evoked in the Fresco. The causes may be plural, according to discussions with students: due to too much or too little playfulness included in the Fresco, and/or because of the complexity of the links between causes and consequences of phenomena, and/or because the Fresco offers no solutions to solve the problems it shows, thus leaving the students in a unpleasant situation of helplessness, and/or because learning such phenomena should rationally lead to changing one's way of life—at least on some dimensions—with some students resisting this aspect. Subsequently, the course positioned itself in continuity with the Fresco, beginning by a revision of several key notions and concepts. Then, since 2023, the Climate Fresco has been replaced by another workshop—the 2 tons one—in order for students to have the opportunity to be proactive towards climate change. Thus, the first sessions of the course are in a process of adaptation to the compulsory programmes offered to all of the students.

The courses offered in the related chairs are more specialized (in finance or circular economy), or more general (on ecological transition) than the *Energy transition stakes* course. Until 2023–2024, the course Energy transition stakes sited in between these two types of offers. From 2024 to 2025, the course will be compulsory for students of the *Ecological transition talents* chair, as it will be useful for these students.

For a reader who is not a teacher nor a professor, this context evolution shows, at the only level of one elective course, the adaptation to be made in order to propose a course that is coherent with the whole evolution of the curricula. Let's imagine the work necessary to adapt a whole programme, thus many courses at the same time, to ecological transition.

Students' profiles

Course student profiles are, as such, very different, for in the master's programme—and with the exception of fundamental and chair courses (for those students that choose to be a member of a chair) that are mandatory—ESSEC students can choose their electives among more than 350 on offer. For an ESSEC master's degree, the usual format is ten sessions, usually one per week, and of 2 hours and 15 minutes each.

Some students come directly from the pre-master year, others are in their third, fourth or fifth year at school and have developed a specialization and experienced several related internships. Other students are new in the school and already possess a master's degree from another institution in a large variety of disciplines. The Energy transition course often includes students having studied engineering of various specializations who want to learn more about energy transition while at the same time taking perspective and leaning on their technical expertise. Moreover, some students are active in student movements and associations. Consequently, the student audience is very varied—as are their expectations.

Business schools have not experienced a student "ecological bifurcation initiative", such as witnessed in the 2022 student graduation speech at AgroParisTech, a French school of agricultural engineering. In this instance, students encouraged others to refuse entering into "business-as-usual" jobs—characterized by over-consumption and waste—and instead bifurcate towards professions that respect and preserve nature. Nevertheless, the students who choose the course have very diverse profiles, motivations and previous knowledge on energy and ecological matters. Indeed, at least a few students each year possess a significant expertise in environmental matters that stems from reading expert reports, media coverage of climate issues, specialized books and also internship experience or work in NGOs. These students have a desire to professionally contribute to protecting the planet and hope to gain additional knowledge and ways to contribute in an impactful way. On the other hand, some students choose the course as an introduction to environmental matters in general or, more specifically, on energy matters. These types of students have had little or no contact with reading matter or experience in the course subject. They are undecided at this stage whether they would commit to actions in favour of the environment in their private and professional life. In between these two extremes, most students have knowledge on some dimensions of the course. Here, this knowledge may come from their previous training as engineers, or legal or finance experts, for examples. It can also come from reading and listening to experts as part of an individual learning process.

Such a variety of students has several important consequences: specific pedagogical methods are required and, as we will see, the professor needs to adopt an adapted stance. However, the track's pedagogical principles—coherent with their objectives—are not only defined to adapt to students profiles. They are first and foremost coherent with the course objectives.

The first course objective through the problematization method

The first course objective is a long-term one: helping students, at the end of the course, to think about energy transition stakes by themselves in a rigorous and open-minded way. Such a capacity seems essential, as transitional and radical changes have to be made at organization level in order to contribute to mitigate and adapt to climate change, biodiversity loss and scarcity of resources. One of the course's basic assumptions made at the beginning is that energy transition, even if it is only one part of the required ecological transition, cannot be taught exhaustively either in a sole course or at only one specific moment during the student experience. Indeed, students will have to learn continually about ecological and energy matters. As such, they need a methodology to practice such a learning process, characterized by a capacity to listen, read diverse and pluralist visions and expertise, and have the capacity to determine the rigour and relevance of each one. While building a virtual dialogue between the holders of such visions and expertise, students will be able to identify their subjects of agreement and of disagreement. Based on this information, students can then form their own vision, progressively develop their own expertise and decide how to contribute to what changes and in which organization. In this way, the methodology also helps students make their own first carrier choices. Such a methodology is well known among researchers in social and management sciences. It is a problematization one.

When students deepen their knowledge of a subject, they automatically use the dialectic method they previously learned: thesis, antithesis and synthesis. But the dialectic method restrains them on several levels. First, the reasoning result is known from scratch: it will be a synthesis. As such, creativity is lost in dialectics. Second, two opposed visions have to be determined regarding any situation. This exercise can have a result of exaggerating oppositions, or creating polarization, in an artificial way in order to create a thesis and an antithesis. Third, synthesis is then perceived as always possible and desirable—that is, the most intelligent way to understand and solve a situation. In fact, the synthesis sometimes only reintegrates the nuances eliminated while creating a thesis and an antithesis. Furthermore, it is not always possible nor desirable to do so, especially in ecological and energy matters. For example, a synthesis between reducing greenhouse gas emissions and pursuing an economic growth measured through GDP can lead to favouring green growth. Such an apparently ideal and seductive synthesis between protecting the Planet and pursuing countries' development (as defined by the GDP) indeed appears in many scenarios (Ramos & Mossé, 2021). However, their hypothesis should be looked at more deeply—as their realism at the required level and speed is unproven.

At the classroom level, the dialectic method transforms itself in a tool for not working collectively: students can divide up their work from scratch, thesis for some and antithesis for others, without discussion nor confrontation of ideas and argument.

In the course, in parallel to the sessions, students have to form groups of three to five and define a subject to problematize progressively. The professor validates the subjects. The topics should of course be related to the energy transition, and be defined at the level of an economic sector at the largest, a group of organizations, a sole organization, or a region in order for them to be anchored in real phenomena, of which the complexity should be revealed. Students send the professor three documents during the course, each time showing a new step in their group work after receiving the professor's comments. The last three sessions are dedicated to group work. The first two mainly include discussions between the professor and each group separately and finish by the professor giving key takeaways for all of them. The last session is dedicated to the group work presentations. Then, each group has to conceive a written report of its work, taking into account the questions and remarks made during the last session. These two deliverables form the core of their evaluation.

Problematizing implies not only working together on the discovered knowledge, but also accepting the insecurity of discovering knowledge without a predefined structure as in the dialectical method. In such a learning-by-doing approach (Dewey, 1916), one can presume that students, once in a working situation, could accept the insecurity of discovering new knowledge on energy transition in potentially unstructured manners. This way, they are able to try to understand the problems they will be confronted with instead of automatically invoking a technical solution to an ill-defined problem.

Finally, business school students are used to working in groups and they know it is a relevant skill for them. The course gives more meaning to such group work. Moreover, these group working sessions are one of the many sharing opportunities offered in the course, as shown in the next paragraph.

The second course objective through sharing as a pedagogical method

In the first session, when presenting the framework and the pedagogical pillars of the course, the importance of sharing and its rationale are explained. First, the theme of the course is transdisciplinary—that is, it covers a large scope of societal phenomena that should be observed and explained by different disciplines. Moreover, for some of them, these phenomena are evolving. Students are therefore encouraged to add relevant information and knowledge at any moment of the course, in addition to their more or less critical questions. Second, some students, especially on ecological and energy matters, know more than the professor does on specific subjects. The professor recognizes and accepts this dimension from the outset and asks students to share their knowledge with all the course participants. In particular, the list of references given by the professor at the beginning of the course grows regularly, be it with films, videos, press articles or expert reports.

Such a sharing way of teaching is indeed possible at master's level, as students are mature enough to understand and accept that the professor is not omniscient.

After the two first sessions presenting basic concepts and phenomena in addition to a synthesis of the history of international agreements on the climate, practitioner guests come and share their experience and expertise with the students. Students dialogue with five guests in each course, one guest representing an economic sector, be it mobility, construction, finance, or energy production to name a few.

Each guest presents the stakes of energy transition in her sector from her point of view, then from the level of her organization and the way they are tackled at a strategic and operational level. She then discusses with the students, in particular regarding the successes attained while not avoiding difficulties and failures. The professor prepares each guest session, presenting the specificity of each class, the already defined concepts, notions and methods while each guest proposes to add others. A 15–20-minute debriefing begins in the next session where students can express themselves on each guest speaker: concepts, notions and methods are revised as appropriate and additional knowledge can be added.

Each course benefits from a student-assistant who writes the minutes of the sessions, including all the knowledge shared by the professor, guests and students. After validation by the professor, the students receive the minutes before the next session. As such, the knowledge available for all progressively grows during the course.

Overall, such a process enhances knowledge, experience sharing and cooperation. Cooperation here is defined as Richard Sennett does (2012), not from a moral point of view, but as a social skill that is disappearing in society along with social rituals, even though it should be learned and practiced in an increasingly complex world. For Sennett, when individuals cooperate, they engage in dialogical interactions based on empathy—that is, attention and sensitivity to others. Dialogical interactions, contrary to dialectics, open up the social space and can lead to unintended positive outcomes.

The social skill dimension of sharing and cooperating regularly appears in the first sessions and debriefings: some of the students ask questions from a critical point of view in an aggressive manner, while others do not, afraid of appearing aggressive. Debriefings constitute a privileged space for students to discuss about their stances towards others, promote freedom of expression and lead students to experiment new forms of questioning. One principal pillar of the course, defined at the beginning but better understood later, is that each student can ask the questions she wants to, on the condition that she provides arguments where appropriate and respects others as individuals even if they might criticize her discourse. Respecting others is a value understood in itself, but it is also learned as the only way to be listened to, and thus answered properly, by others. In sum, the classroom offers a collective learning process for students' assertiveness.

As for the cooperation dimension enhanced by Sennett, sharing can be conceived as one dimension of Dewey's pragmatist view on pedagogy: in order for young people to be able to make their way creatively and responsively in the world, they must be involved collectively in thinking and trying to invent remedies to societal problems from the moment they begin their studies.

Indeed, through working in class and in groups, students enhance cooperation, dialogue and debate between potentially divergent parties—much like the discussions students should take part in while later working in companies; and in order to contribute to the energy transition in particular, and other complex subjects in general. The course is thus designed as an experimentation of a collective reflection and action.

In such a course format, the professor adopts a specific stance: she plays the role of a guarantor, a coach and a non-omniscient expert. She is not the omniscient expert that conveys knowledge and skills to students. And her status in the classroom is neither the same as the students', teaching in a totally horizontal and potentially demagogic vision of pedagogy (de Carlo, 2005, 2012).

The professor guarantees the institution's rules as well as ensuring that everyone is treated with respect in the classroom. Any opinion given must be based on arguments and, if possible, on precise references. Moreover, any type of question can be asked to the guests, the condition being that guests listen and receive the questions without closing themselves up when faced with "aggression". As such, the course is also an opportunity for the students to experiment how to express potential divergence in content while avoiding being aggressive to others nor abandoning their questions through fear of being aggressive. The beginning of each session, before the guests speaks, is a privileged moment to talk about this required dialogic stance, introduced as a change tool. As multiparty decision processes are needed to define and organize the ecological and energy transition, students have to know how to contribute to dialogue involving very different stakeholders.

Moreover, the professor plays the role of a coach to accompany students in their group work and to facilitate classroom discussions. And, more traditionally, she passes on knowledge to her students.

Such a professor's stance implies that students can develop—as indeed they are encouraged to do so—their own world vision, potentially different from that of the professor. The professor does not assess the course success by counting the number of students who adhere to her own vision, nor the depth to which they adhere to it. There is no consensus in the class and students simultaneously develop different visions of the world. The main objective for the professor is that students should be rigorous in their reasoning and take into account pluralistic arguments. It is worth noting that students progressively develop their knowledge and capacity for criticism—and that they are not all at the same phase of the process at the same time.

The professor does not pretend to be neutral. She has her own world vision. When she talks about it, she informs the students that she is doing so, distinguishing the status of the given information.

Like in the teaching experience of Acquier and Pereytou (2022), students anonymously provide course assessments situated between 4 and 5 out of 5. These are good assessments, meaning that most of the students appreciate the course, and this confirms the collective discussion that took place in the last session. Students say, and/or write to the professor on how they appreciate the phenomena and knowledge they learned, as well as the personal and organizational engagements they discovered stemming from very different sources: professor, guests, readings, working together, etc. Regularly, students benefit from this learning process for internships, specialized diplomas or first jobs.

Nevertheless, the course does not receive 4.9 out of 5 assessments, such as for some popular courses. At least three explanations can be cited. First, international research—whatever the course delivered—shows that female professors' courses are always more badly assessed than male professors' courses. Second, as students develop their critical thinking in the course, they use it in their assessments. Third, as problematizing is a very demanding exercise, some students who did not give enough energy or reflexion to it can, *a posteriori*, rationalize dissatisfaction by adapting their assessment to it. In particular, the problematization exercise often confronts the preconceived vision that techno-solutionism can alone save the Planet and some students would prefer, or feel compelled to, stay in such a vision. In their

Energy transition course at ESCP Business School in Paris, Profs. Acquier and Pereytou also found that students tend to internalize the "imperatives" of economic growth (2022).

The third course objective through passing on content to the students

How can a chapter on a course on the *Energy transition stakes* only talk about its content in the last part of it? Especially after explaining pedagogical choices giving prime place to methods and stances that are not specific to energy transition matters?

An underlying objective of the course is that students will be more motivated to commit themselves as actors in the energy transition, while not necessarily knowing all the foundations of knowledge and skills. While committed, they will learn more if they possess a methodology to do so, and if they want to. Thus, knowledge and skills are conceived in the course in an instrumental way—that is, as tools useful for change.

One might ask if a course regarding energy transition stakes in a business school should teach a maximum number of concepts, notions and methods. Should it not be compulsory to do so? It depends on the importance we give to the phenomena "energy transition". If it is possible to make such a transition (Freyssoz, 2024), it will come through the motivation and initiatives of young ones, part of them possessing useful knowledge. And a professor finds what is useful to know regarding energy transition knowledge in her expertise and in public reports.

However, she has to remain modest regarding the real impact of this knowledge on the commitment of her students. Indeed, it is defined by older adults who are experts in their respective fields, deciding for young adults what they should know, and in a process they conceive as one of conveying the sense of immutable continuity (Mead, 1971, quoted by Foray, 2022). Older adults do so mostly unconsciously. Mead encourages professors to distance themselves from what they want to teach. And every day one can observe that possessing knowledge on ecological matters is not enough in itself to engage a change process at the individual or organizational level.

What about specialized skills? An energy transition course could use business cases in order to teach students how to change a business model in an energy saving way. At the time of this course, that is, 25 hours only, the choice was made to invite experts in the field who themselves present the stakes and evolving situation of their company or territory regarding energy. At the same time, they define their occupations and are a source of inspiration for the students who often discover new professions.

Once the relative status of possessing knowledge and skills discussed, it is still relevant to pass on some knowledge to the students before any discussion develops in class. In the first two sessions of the course, energy is defined in a very accessible way: a physic entity defined by its effects—that is, to produce heat or induce a movement (Gayvallet, 2019). The effect of greenhouse gases, the carbon cycle, sources and carbon sinks, and the notions of adaptation to versus mitigation of climate change represent the very few concepts defined at the beginning of the course. Even the first and second principles of thermodynamics are not defined in the first two sessions. They are indeed often evoked in discussions to explain concrete phenomena, though much of the time they are not presented as thermodynamics principles.

The reason for this choice is not only that students are more interested in learning a definition when it is useful to understand a subject they want to explore. It is also because some of them also decided to choose economic and commercial preparatory classes in order to avoid physics and chemistry after high school.

The first two sessions offer a rapid history of international treaties on the environment and climate. It situates the creation of IPCC and the weight and rationales of the different stakeholders in international decisions. The role of some important lobbies is explained through the evocation of Oreskes and Conway's (2011) work on "Merchants of doubt". The result is that students improve their understanding of the necessity to refer to rigorous sources and to clearly distinguish between a quotation and a personal or collective reflexion—the only way to take distance with greenwashing practices that some of them denounce strongly.

Many other concepts, notions and methods relevant to various economic sectors take place in guests' presentations and in classroom debates. The professor trusts the classroom discussions in order to give her the opportunity of defining the concepts she wants to teach, from the difference between low and high sustainability to the principle and interest of water electrolysis, through energy efficiency and sobriety. The first guest typically presents and explains the French electricity system, its history and current players, the main concepts necessary to handle it, and the stakes this system has to deal with in a period of electrification of activities and the multiplication of producers. These changes have strong consequences in terms of management and are part of the context for many economic activities.

Future developments

This chapter has attempted to offer a pragmatic approach to designing a course on Energy transition stakes in a Master of Management programme at a French business school. Without being a model, the course plays the role in this book of an opportunity to introduce pedagogical questions and stakes in the teaching of ecological matters in business schools. In the course approach, the students' learning process takes precedence over the passing on of content from the professor to the students. The professor adapts the course and her sessions in order for knowledge to be vectored as a discovery, requested by the students rather than given at the professor's preferred moment.

Thanks to the growing number of involved professors and institutions (The Shift Project & Audencia, 2022), fruitful discussions and dialogue are developing on the teaching of ecological matters in business schools. One of the next steps is to develop its pedagogy even further.

Key takeaways:

- Ecological transition in higher education should encompass the subject's complexity through interdisciplinarity and lead to the redesign of the entire range of programmes and courses of schools and universities.
- The objective is long-term: helping students to think about energy transition stakes by themselves in a rigorous and open-minded way. This is essential, as transitional and radical changes have to be made at organization level in order to contribute to mitigate and adapt to climate change, biodiversity loss and scarcity of resources
- Students have to learn continually about ecological and energy matters and need a capacity to listen, read diverse and pluralist visions and expertise, and have the capacity to determine the rigour and relevance of each one.
- Students can then form their own vision, progressively develop their own expertise and decide how to contribute to what changes and in which organization. In this way, the methodology also helps students make their own first carrier choices.
- Problematizing implies not only working together on the discovered knowledge, but also accepting the insecurity of discovering knowledge without a predefined structure such as in the dialectical method.
- Some students, especially on ecological and energy matters, know more than the professor does on specific subjects.
- Each student should be allowed to ask the questions she wants to, on the condition that she provides arguments where appropriate and respects others as individuals even if they might criticize her discourse.
- The professor adopts a specific stance, playing the role of a guarantor, a coach and a non-omniscient expert.
- As multiparty decision processes are needed to define and organize the ecological and energy transition, students have to know how to contribute to dialogue involving very different stakeholders.
- The professor does not assess the course success by counting the number of students who adhere to her own vision, nor the depth to which they adhere to it. There is no consensus in the class and students simultaneously develop different visions of the world.
- The professor does not pretend to be neutral. She has her own world vision. When she talks about it, she informs the students that she is doing so, distinguishing the status of the given information.

Food for thought:

- To what extent should the subject of energy transition be made mandatory in all teaching? And at what level? Why?

- In the ESSEC example, the professor takes on a role of coach and facilitator in the classroom. To what extent have you experienced such an approach during your studies and what did you like or dislike about it?
- Can the students themselves take on the role of providers of knowledge and complement the professor? Can they substitute her? What would the pros and cons of such methods be?
- The importance of dialogue in a more and more polarized society is invoked in this chapter regarding energy transition stakes. What are, according to you, polarized subjects regarding energy and why?

References

Aurélien, A., & Peyretou, P. (2022, May 20). How to teach energy transition and climate in business schools. *International Science Council Blog*. International Science Council.pdf

Collectif FORTES. (2020). *Manuel de la grande transition*. Les Liens qui libèrent.

de Carlo, L. (2005). Accepting conflict and experiencing creativity: Teaching “concertation” using La Francilienne CD ROM. *Negotiation Journal*, *21*(1), 85–103.

de Carlo, L. (2012). Teaching negotiation through paradox. *Negotiation Journal*, *28*(3), 351–364.

de Carlo, L. (2013). Teaching a common good in a business school: The ESSEC seminar on Water Management. In S. Gröschl (Dir.), *Uncertainty, diversity and social responsibility* (pp. 181–194). Grower Publishing.

de Carlo, L. (2020, June 8). Management: Enseigner l’action collective pour la transition écologique. *The Conversation France*. https://theconversation.com/management-enseigner-laction-collective-pour-la-transition-ecologique-139536

Dewey, J. (1916). *Democracy and education* (p. 434). The Macmillan Company.

Foray, P. (2022, January 6). Le fossé des générations, un défi pour la transmission éducative. *The Conversation France*. Le fossé des générations, un défi pour la transmission éducative.pdf

Freyssoz, J.-B. (2024). Sans transition-Une nouvelle histoire de l’énergie. Le Seuil.

Gayvallet, H. (2019). L’énergie-Aspects généraux. In *Cultures sciences physiques*. ENS Lyon. http://culturesciencesphysique.ens-lyon.fr/ressource/Energie.xml

Jouzel, J. (groupe de travail sous la direction de). (2022). Sensibiliser et former aux enjeux de la transition écologique et du développement durable dans l’enseignement supérieur. In *Rapport à Frédérique Vidal, Ministre de l’enseignement supérieur, de la recherche et de l’innovation*. Février. www.enseignementsup-recherche.gouv.fr/sites/default/files/2022-02/rapport-former-aux-enjeux-de-la-transition-ecologique-dans-l-es-pdf-16808.pdf

Oreskes, N., & Conway, E. M. (2011). *Merchants of doubt*. Bloomsbury Publishing.

Ramos, C., & Mossé, J. (2021). Découplage et croissance verte. *Carbone 4*. www.carbone4.com/publication-decouplage

Sennett, R. (2012). Together: The rituals, pleasures and politics of cooperation. Yale University Press (French Translation: Ensemble: Pour une éthique de la coopération, Paris: Albin Michel, 2014).

The Shift Project and Audencia. (2022, November). *Former les acteurs de l’économie de demain*. Rapport Final, Paris. https://theshiftproject.org/wp-content/uploads/2023/02/230214-ClimatSup-Business-Rapport-final-The-Shift-Project.pdf

Von der Leyen, U. (2022). *Proposal for a council recommendation on learning for environmental sustainability*. European Commission. https://eur-lex.europa.eu/legal-content/EN/TXT/PDF/?uri=CELEX:52022DC0011

10 When French public hospitals go green?

Reworking the boundaries of hospital practices

Marie-Léandre Gomez and Marion Ligonie

Mens sana in corpore sano . . . in planeta sana

Scientific and medical research pointing to the impact of pollutants on human health confirms that a healthy body and a healthy mind cannot simply *exist* without a healthy planet. We are increasingly aware that the health of humans—if not their survival—depends on ecological sustainability. The Lancet Countdown on health and climate change reports an increase by 54% of heat-related deaths in older people in the last two decades and more than 1 million premature deaths due to air pollution from coal-fired power in 2018. Hospitals, for example, are energy intensive, consume large amounts of clean water, use frightening quantities of disposable equipment, most of it plastic-made, and release highly polluting waste. Their environmental footprint accounts for up to 5% of the global footprint (in France, 3.19%). They use 1.5% of scarce water in the world and produce 4.4% of total greenhouse gas emissions. This is a paradox for healthcare organizations: while they are the guarantors of human health, they also are among the planet's greatest polluters.

Faced with increasing popular and institutional pressures to change, healthcare organizations have begun to implement environmentally friendly, socially responsible practices. Still, their initiatives have remained nascent. In 2016, in France, less than 7% of hospitals answered the first National Observatory on Sustainable Development, showing their meagre interest for the topic. Most respondents were also at an early stage, with an average maturity grade of 38%. However, some hospitals managed to get to a more advanced stage. How could Sustainable Development (SD) practices develop in such refractory organizations? How could SD managers and hospital directors willing to extend SD strategies move forward?

Using the concept of boundary work, we can understand the implementation of SD practices in French hospitals, where much inertia and even some forms of opposition slow down their development. Boundary work corresponds to the "effort to influence the social, symbolic, material, or temporal boundaries; demarcations; and distinctions affecting groups, occupations, and organizations" (Langley et al., 2019). Understanding the boundary work performed

DOI: 10.4324/9781003522355-14

to develop SD practices in hospitals can help foster SD in other industries facing such reluctance.

The challenges of an ecological transition in healthcare: friends or foes?

In organizations, the ecological transition is often addressed as part of sustainable development (SD) practices. According to the Bruntland report (1987), SD is defined as a "development that meets the need of the present without compromising the ability of future generations to meet their own needs". It encourages organizations to accommodate stakeholders' expectations and limit the negative impacts generated by their activities. As the author and entrepreneur John Elkington notes, environmental issues stand as one of the essential pillars of SD, alongside social, societal, economic, and ethical matters.

In theory, SD is largely compatible with hospitals' missions. Healthcare practices are fuelled by practitioners' moral commitment to promote people's well-being and to care for the community. Moreover, SD and the ecological transition appear as intrinsic to these purposes given the well-documented consequences of environmental degradations on people's health, on social inequalities, and on the well-being of populations. Inversely, hospitals' "inside-out impacts" play a part in the ecological decline and makes them accountable for their impact. Finally, SD as a whole is put forward as a solution to the soaring health costs and bankrupt French social security system, and is viewed as an opportunity to align economic efficiency with an accrued attention to social commitments.

Despite such promises, the implementation of SD practices remains perilous in hospitals. In addition to constraints on resources, these practices add to already complex organizations. This is because in hospitals, like elsewhere, SD creates the need for new governance systems capable of respecting the diversity of interests at stake, new human resource policies and, above all, dynamics of learning, innovation, and continuous adaptation. Even when they are coherent with medical practitioners' personal values, SD practices are impeded by strong professional identities that depreciate subjective value-driven decisions while encouraging "scientific" objectivity and a procedural culture focused on efficiency and easily measurable outcomes.

Given these issues, SD implementation in French hospitals remains relatively understudied. Research has mostly focused on technical aspects of the healthcare ecological transition, examining architectural features of hospital buildings or technological advances in energy and water use reduction. Meanwhile, it has overlooked the socio-organizational factors at play, especially when considering the practice of medicine itself.

Yet the specificities of the French health sector preclude the import of integration strategies and methods from other sectors. Firstly, to cite Fabrizio Russo (2016), "the status of the patient is ontologically different from that of the customer and postulates a different approach to that of other types of organisations". Secondly, the organizational functioning of hospitals is made unique by complex administrative procedures, increasingly specialized professionals whose tasks must be coordinated, and a predominant focus on patients and their needs. In such a setting, SD raises issues specific to French public hospitals that limit the applicability of existing knowledge on its implementation in other contexts. As such, we draw attention to the boundary work of internal and external actors when striving to develop SD practices.

Boundary work for SD practices

Boundary work refers to the "purposeful individual and collective effort to influence the social, symbolic, material, or temporal boundaries; demarcations; and distinctions affecting groups, occupations, and organizations" (Langley et al., 2019, p. 704). Boundary work focuses primarily on the negotiations, tensions, and cooperation that perpetuate or transform boundaries between groups and/or practices. Zietsma and Lawrence (2010) distinguish between boundary work—efforts to maintain or change boundaries between groups and/or practices—and practice work—efforts to stabilize or transform the practices themselves—the combination of which produces institutional work.

Langley et al. identified three types of boundary work. Competitive boundary work occurs when actors defend, contest, or create boundaries in order to gain legitimacy and power. It focuses on the frictions generated by the coexistence of diverse groups, occupations or practices. In contrast, collaborative boundary work highlights how boundaries can be negotiated, accommodated or mitigated to facilitate cooperation and the achievement of collective goals. Last, configurational boundary work shapes boundaries to make new activities possible, by modifying interactions, creating neutral spaces where divergent interests can reconcile, or uniting existing activities.

Past studies have documented that SD supposes multi-level boundary work. At the organizational level, SD redefines organizational boundaries in order to incorporate stakeholders' expectations in their business models. Within organizations, the strategic integration of SD requires intense boundary work to align, legitimize, and stabilize the practice among other organizational practices. Acquier et al. (2018) show that in the subsidiary of a multinational company, SD implementation involved both intra- and inter-organizational boundary work. Intra-organizational boundary work required the help of actors mastering the codes of several practices, the presence of champions within the management team, and the creation of multi-skilled teams. Inter-organizational work combined participation in projects with other industry players, building partnerships and moving from a company-focused view to being open to the whole value chain.

French healthcare organizations are also the sites of documented boundary work. The diversity of occupations coexisting in hospitals (nursing assistants, nurses, doctors of various specialities, administrative staff) gives rise to more or less conflictual negotiations of the boundaries between groups. Moreover, boundary work is crucial when new practices are established in hospitals, especially since they are characterized by frequent technological innovations that often require some boundary work to remodel and/or maintain the balance of powers and interactions.

As such, boundary work appears as an essential ingredient both to the implementation of new SD practices and to the running of hospitals. So how does SD-related boundary work occur in hospitals?

A study of French hospitals

We studied two national-level organizations (a leading professional organization and *Agence Nationale d'Appui à la Performance des établissements de santé et médico-sociaux* (ANAP)[1]) to understand the context of SD in the French healthcare sector and to identify the most advanced players on the subject. We then selected four public hospitals which stood out as more proactive on SD matters. We collected data mainly through interviews with SD managers in each hospital and with relevant actors in national-level organizations. We also observed meetings and analysed documents, both internal to the hospitals (hospitals projects and strategic plans, SD action plans, internal communication documents) and external (press articles, feedback, websites of institutional players).

The greening of French public hospitals

The first development of SD in French hospitals were local initiatives in a very limited number of hospitals in the early 2000s. Figure 10.1 highlights the main advances of SD in healthcare at the international and French level.

The few French hospitals developing responsible practices could do so thanks to the combined impetus of hospital directors wishing to promote the ecological transition of their organization, and SD managers who quickly understood that the challenge was at the national level too. Indeed, they played a driving role in the institutional development of SD practices in the French hospital sector. Firstly, they pushed the internal boundaries within their respective hospitals to federate the efforts of willing employees. Secondly, they worked to push the boundaries at the field level, aware that without a change in the boundaries at the field level, they would quickly be blocked within their organizations. To do this, they cooperated and acted together and enabled the development of institutional policies. Thirdly, they pushed the traditional organizational boundaries of hospitals and relied on an external network in their local area to enable the emergence of new shared practices with nearby companies and local authorities, performing collaborative boundary work.

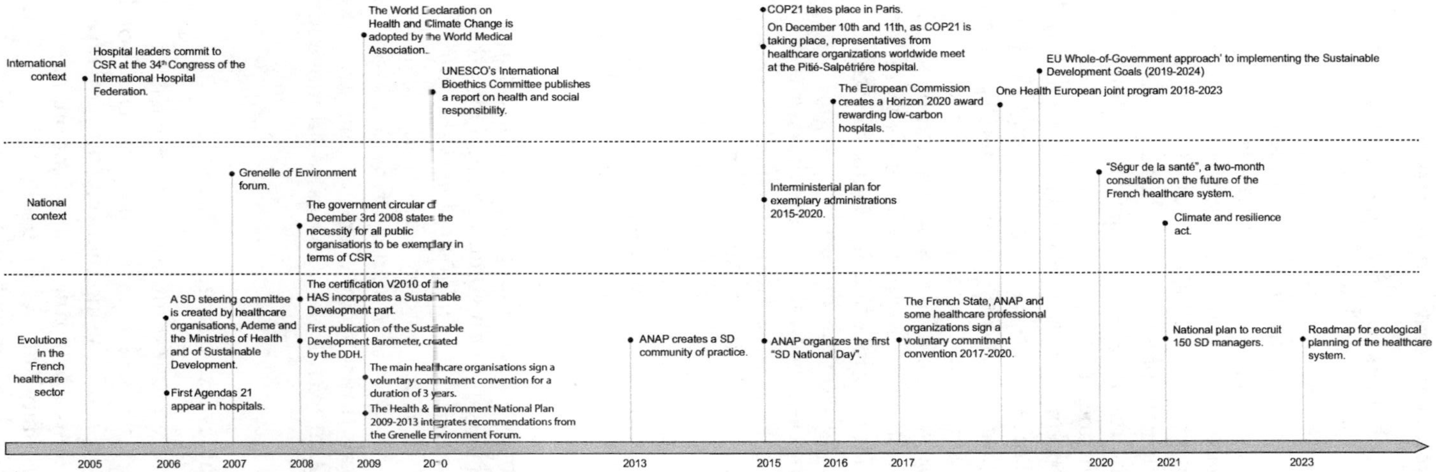

Figure 10.1 Main events leading to Corporate Social Responsibility (CSR) development in French hospitals

Internal competitive and cooperative boundary work

As most SD hospital managers have no dedicated team, they rely on the creation of volunteering networks to develop SD practices. These volunteers propose new projects and communicate on existing projects in order to mobilize more people, and to enhance the development of SD practices. Most of the projects first refer to improving waste management and decrease water and energy consumption. These projects contribute to moving the frontiers between medical departments and non-medical departments and easily find support to implement new practices. The heads of departments and hospitals' directors give the resources needed, as these projects also contribute to decreasing costs in the medium run.

It is important to point out that boundaries are more difficult to move when ecological practices are seen as contradicting traditional care or medical practices. Ecological practices have to demonstrate that they are not medically equivalent, but even better, and that they are not more expensive. This has been the case with an initiative on apitherapy for chronical wounds. It had to demonstrate that the medical outcomes were better than conventional medicine, with more rapid healing. Being four times cheaper was also a strong argument to develop this project.

In the cases we studied, medical doctors—in particular heads of medical departments—are considered the most difficult to involve. They sometimes block the development of initiatives, considering that they don't create value for the patient. Among the few doctors mobilized before the Covid-19 crisis, the head of the anaesthesiology-resuscitation department in a large hospital developed a project aiming to decrease the use of anaesthesiologic gases which have terrible environmental impact, being both polluting and toxic. This project had also to demonstrate that the cost was lower.

The SD managers we interviewed all consider that they could not have developed new practices without the support of their hospital director. They also all see the limits in relying on volunteers, and already motivated people: "*once the most motivated, those who were already convinced, as citizens of the importance to change, are involved, it is really difficult to get the others moving*" (interview M, R). As a matter of fact, a group of SD managers from different hospitals turned to moving the boundaries at the institutional level, with the view that even locally, things could move forward only with a global move.

Acting at the national level to change practices

These SD managers acted as institutional entrepreneurs and performed configurational boundary work that made SD a practice for hospitals at the national level. While in 2005, the international hospital directors' association claimed that "the hospital, by virtue of its vocation, missions and activities, has a greater responsibility and a duty to set an example in the implementation of a sustainable development strategy", only a few French hospitals were actively developing SD. The *Grenelle de l'Environnement*—a set of high-level meetings in France aiming to make long-term decisions regarding the environment and sustainable development—of 2007 was followed by a governmental decision that all public organizations, including hospitals, should develop an SD plan and submit it to the French Prime Minister. The small group of hospitals' SD managers convinced the national agency for hospital performance, ANAP, to create a Sustainable Development Group, in order to help hospitals to move forward (interview with ANAP managers). They negotiated the creation of an official community of practice inside the agency, as for other occupations such as financial directors, supply managers, to cite a few. The agency implemented a national observatory and began to advise hospitals willing to develop SD policies. It was also during the years 2017–2020 that environmental concerns arose in hospitals. In 2021, in the context of a new national development plan for hospitals (*Segur de la Santé*), it was decided to fund the recruitment of 150 SD managers.

Medical doctors willing to change the practices also turned to the institutional level to obtain support and leverage the practice. In the case of the aforementioned anaesthesiologist, he presented the use of the alternative to toxic gas to the powerful medical association of his specialty, created an SD group inside this association and set up a series of dedicated scientific days. Doctors' training is some hospitals may now also include some hours on SD in medical practices.

Collaborative boundary work between hospitals and local organizations

As SD managers found limited support inside hospitals, they turned to find allies and partners outside the hospitals—in the local civil service, public agencies or local businesses. This is rather original in French hospital culture, which traditionally remains behind the hospitals' frontiers. This collaborative boundary work was all the more natural for the SD managers who worked in companies or local authorities of the area before joining the hospital. For example, in Niort, there is a committee on sustainable development, which includes all the major organizations and companies in the area. It meets twice a year. Partners also try to work together on new perimeters: purchasing, mobility, and printing.

> We held a mobility day together. We have common problems, with a travel plan. We [in hospitals] work days and nights, weekends and public holidays . . . On a subject like this, we all have to work together, especially with the conurbation, for public transport, journeys and timetables. It's important to work with them and with the companies that have the same problems. The hospital alone in its territory, isolated and deciding on its own, is over.
>
> (Interview with the SD manager of the Niort hospital)

In further stages, hospital managers also involved their suppliers and sub-contractors in developing their green policies.

Rethinking the boundaries within and across hospitals

Within a sector where most actors remain reluctant or passive regarding the development of SD practices, actors who try to move forward have to make the frontiers between activities, groups, occupations, and organizations more porous. They perform various types of boundary work, in order to negotiate new alliances, inside their organizations—with organizations at the national level, and with local organizations. While boundary work has been reported in hospitals, in particular to develop medical innovation, with SD we were able to observe forms of boundary work involving those of the organizations, and in order to bypass these boundaries inside the organization.

Key takeaways:

- SD implementation in hospitals is complex due to resource constraints, professional identities, and the need for new governance systems, human resource policies, and continuous adaptation. Understanding the boundary work involved can help overcome these challenges.
- Internal competitive and cooperative boundary work is essential in mobilizing hospital employees, creating volunteering networks, and developing SD projects. Collaboration between SD managers, hospital directors, and departments is crucial for resource allocation and overcoming resistance.
- SD managers also act as institutional entrepreneurs to promote SD practices at the national level. They play a driving role in influencing policy development and creating a supportive environment for SD initiatives in healthcare organizations.
- The greening of French public hospitals, so far, has been facilitated by the combined impetus of hospital directors, SD managers, and external networks, leading to the development of local initiatives and shared practices with nearby companies and authorities.

Food for thought:

- Think of your country. To what extent has the health system undertaken initiatives to reduce the negative impact of hospitals on the environment? What tangible changes have been made?
- A competitive boundary occurs when employees defend, contest, or create boundaries in order to gain legitimacy and power. To what extent is this a feature of your own organization or institution? What impact does it have on projects and initiatives, or simply the need to "get things done"?
- Some view sustainable development as a "nice to have" or even something that is of secondary importance in an organization. However, in the case

of hospitals SD has been seen to be useful and effective in moving towards the transition. Why is it that SD evokes these contradictory perceptions?

Note

1 ANAP is a public agency in charge of accompanying hospitals in their organizational and managerial development.

References

Acquier, A., Carbone, V., & Moatti, V. (2018). "Teaching the Sushi Chef": Hybridization work and CSR integration in a Japanese multinational company. *Journal of Business Ethics*, *148*(3), 625–645.

Langley, A., Lindberg, K., Mørk, B. E., Nicolini, D., Raviola, E., & Walter, L. (2019). Boundary work among groups, occupations, and organizations: From cartography to process. *Academy of Management Annals*, *13*(2), 704–736.

Russo, F. (2016). What is the CSR's focus in healthcare? *Journal of Business Ethics*, *134*(2), 323–334.

Zietsma, C., & Lawrence, T. B. (2010). Institutional work in the transformation of an organizational field: The interplay of boundary work and practice work. *Administrative Science Quarterly*, *55*(2), 189–221.

11 How environmental shareholder activism spurs large corporations to communicate on their environmental commitment?

Viviane de Beaufort

Leaders and Corporate Boards are struggling to make climate risk an item on the agenda in France. This is highlighted in a survey carried out by the French Institute of Board Directors with their members and in collaboration with the French energy and climate challenges consultancy Carbone 4. Indeed, the Eurogroup Consulting "corporate barometer" in January 2019 shows that climate risk is only a concern for 24% of CEOs in large French companies.

The gulf between the reality of major risks that leading companies are concerned by, and its weak concrete consideration among management processes and governance, is striking: only 48% of those responding to the Institut Français des Administrateurs survey confirmed that their company boards of directors had set GHG emission reduction objectives. In this context, the rise of an environmental shareholder activism and its role of "meddler" to influence un-proactive boards is an important issue.

Three years ago, we outlined the profile of a new form of shareholder engagement in Europe taking into account the players, their methods, and the themes raised.[1] Since then, we have continued research linked to the EU shareholder rights2 directive, reproduced in France through the PACTE Law, and furthered our work on the social impact dimension of activism in France that is progressively unfolding. If activism is a newcomer to continental shareholder culture, it is becoming structured and taking on the role of a channel of influence which leaders can no longer refuse to pay heed to—be it through dialogue or more incisive ways. For the most part, it takes place through questions during general assemblies—easier to use as a means than submitting resolutions that require gathering a sizeable percentage of voting rights (0.5%–5% according to Article R. 225–71 of the Commercial Law).

Questioning enables specific topics to be raised while giving public exposure to attract citizen and consumer attention, even outside the company. As such, the art of the question is setting itself up as an alternative to more constraining instruments or the option of dispute. In this way, minority shareholders, joining together, attempt to influence the choices of the management team regarding issues that are of concern, among them that of the environment.

While, as minority shareholders, the opportunities to change corporate ESG practices are limited—and the threat of withdrawing investment through

DOI: 10.4324/9781003522355-15

selling their shares has no real impact—Phitrust (an ESG investment firm) and the FIR (*Forum pour l'Investissement Responsible—Forum for Responsible Investment*) use the following levers of influence:

1. systematic direct dialogue with Presidents or CEOs;
2. submitting written resolutions and questions upstream of general assemblies;
3. alerting investors and the wider public through the media;
4. having a presence in the general assemblies of CAC40 companies and systematically voting.

Since 2020, the FIR has launched a series of campaigns for action during general assemblies. We carried out relative research regarding these in 2021, comparing it to the first campaign in 2020 and in expectancy of that of 2022, and present the results hereafter under the theme of ECOLOGY. The "say on climate" practice, which has emerged since 2020, is still too much in its early days to draw an informed lesson, and we shall invoke this in the concluding outlook on future developments.

The rise of shareholder democracy as a driving force for ESG

Shareholder life in the big corporations seems to be shaped by a trend that is akin to that of the citizen in our democracies—with vague hopes of transparency and structured dialogue—notably centring around consultations such as key debates or the conference on the future of Europe. And, if the large US funds in their time consolidated the theory of agency—where the leader is responsible with regard to investors as an agent in charge of taking care of their investments—a wider understanding on the vocation of a company, brought into force by the modification of Civil Law,[2] now leads CEOs to question their activity in light of social, societal, and environmental terms and the firm's impact on climate change and biodiversity. While the traditional topics for question time during general assemblies still live on, they are losing ground to CSR. Moreover, whereas legislators are increasingly creating frameworks for these topics (e.g. the duty of vigilance) that have become factors of strategic risk, activist shareholders are becoming harbingers, at least warning companies of reputational risk.

In parallel to the diversification of activism topics, we can observe a diversification of actors and methods: the discreet but effective traditional influence of the banks, using CSR criteria integrated in their investment policies and supplemented by those of small shareholders, work together via the advice of activist proxies or ESG funds. Even NGOs buy shares to be able to have a voice in board assemblies. Issues raised by the FIR in the series of 2021 General Assemblies that questioned the big CAC40 groups were selected in order to assess the degree of priority large French companies grant to environmental matters. Questioning on the pertinence of the issues addressed by the FIR and the groups' response processes complete the work. Maximising the impact of this action, again undertaken by the FIR in 2022 and aiming for full deployment, was the end-objective of this.

The methodology behind the questions

Work was carried out between April 2021 and April 2022 during the Women Board Ready initiative at ESSEC Business School within the framework of the "sustainable company governance" programme run by the ESSEC *Centre Européen de Droit et Economie*. Three of the 13 written questions related to the environment. The groups' answers were compared to annual corporate reports, as well as CEOs' declarations in the press, reports and comments from NGOs, the standpoint of ESG funds, including that of Phitrust,[3] the Axylia[4] benchmark, and the previous FIR report for 2020,[5] in order to assess their pertinence. The drafts come in the form of Excel files and a CERESSEC[6] working paper was finalised.

Questions linked to ecology posed by the FIR to the CAC40 and assessment of company replies

Question 1—Climate: "To be aligned with the Paris Agreement, what capital expenditure (capex) will you commit to from now until 2025? How is this expenditure distributed throughout the value chain between maintenance capex and growth capex?"

Which companies stand out in the replies?

Good practices can be found in groups that have defined a clear strategy, an action plan and specified capex that tends to prove that tangible steps are underway. Generally, in these groups the environment has been taken into account for some years and has transformed into a real lever for development. Scopes 1 and 2 are particularly well documented. For some companies, implication in scope 3 seems even natural. Bad practices are often correlated with an absence of or lack of communication—for example, on the subject of the capex: no clear corporate strategy, lack of precise and quantitative data, and description of only a few, isolated steps to include ecology on the agenda.

Top BEST

HERMES INTERNATIONAL describes a very clear strategy together with an action plan and specified capex that seems to prove that a concrete global approach is being implemented. The same applies to SCHNEIDER ELECTRIC and the taking into account of the issue of the environment for several years has become a real lever for development. This is a very differentiating asset in comparison with its competitors today. SAINT-GOBAIN also announces a clear and well-documented strategy for scopes 1 and 2 (site operations), but also scope 3 with the taking into account of the impact of the products they offer. In the same way, the implication of the environmental issue in scope 3 is linked to a former positioning in the renovation of buildings. DANONE, the only official mission-driven company, distinguishes itself by assisting agricultural producers—Danone's primary suppliers—which creates a major societal impact.

Flops

Facing these pioneers whose commitment is obvious and who clearly express it with structured, and continuously improved reporting is a "top flop"—ALSTHOM. The company, as in 2020, communicates on nothing, and seems unconcerned by climate-related issues. PUBLICIS, which as a service provider indicates that the subject isn't relevant to it. This is false—at least for the buildings the company is located in—and makes no proposals, as opposed to banks, to indicate what could be considered relevant in its sector of activity. Finally, STELLANTIS provides no specific information, mentioning the possible shift to an electric vehicle fleet but without stating at what date and without indicating anything on energy efficiency—despite their production sites being large consumers. Concerning RENAULT, there is a lack of precise quantitative data and while several isolated approaches have been mentioned, it is very difficult to draw any lessons for a global action plan.

Question 2 Biodiversity: "How do you limit the impact of loss of biodiversity on your future revenues? Specify the indicators and means put in place".

Which companies stand out in the replies?

The top three companies have developed a global strategy to restore biodiversity, and which comes within the scope of a collective approach for action. They are notably aiming to shift the entire value chain to create impact and change beyond their own perimeter. Bad practices can be found in companies which have taken no measures on biodiversity, either considering that their business models are not adapted, or quite simply forgetting this dimension in their environmental policy.

It should be highlighted that the regulatory part around biodiversity is far from being as mature as for other fields, even if the EU has begun to work on the subject, and even if it represents an additional difficulty to assess the pertinence of every company's approach and measure their impact on the protection of biodiversity.[7]

Top best

KERING, with strong engagement to net zero on biodiversity from now until 2025 with the protection of one million hectares of essential and unreplaceable natural habitat—outside their own supply chain—and support for regenerative agriculture practices for a million hectares which, this time, are directly linked to its value chain. Kering has created the *Kering Generating fund for nature* with an envelope of €5m. The group has also set up an EPL financial statement that has been available on open source since 2019. DANONE works concretely for the preservation and development of local and rare varieties in their products. Since 1992, they have been engaged in protecting impluvium with farmers, associations, and public authorities (protection of fragile wetlands through practices). In 2019, the company triggered the creation of the coalition *One planet business for Biodiversity* that brings together 26 large companies. With their partners and suppliers, the group have been behind the setting up of regenerative agricultural systems, which, in 2012, represented 15% of the agricultural ingredients in their products. HERMES INTERNATIONAL has developed partnerships and is part of international initiatives, including *Act4Nature,* that relies on NGOs such as the WWF and Global Biodiversity. The company also refers to the score advocated by the IPBES (Intergovernmental science policy platform on biodiversity and ecosystem service), the equivalent of the IPCC on Biodiversity. Hermès works on multiple operational scenarios in parallel and with a desire not to confine itself to following one sole approach.

Flops

Given its model of diversified business bank, the SOCIETE GENERALE considers its impact on future revenues very limited. Yet this seems to be evidence to the contrary, and, if required, the difficult debate on European taxonomy demonstrates that the decision to finance or not certain companies and sectors has a direct impact on their development. As such, and far from being neutral, the decision to choose to serve companies contributing to biodiversity, or those with a negative impact, directs financial flow towards those who are virtuous and make an effort. ALSTOM does not seem concerned given the following formulated reply: "The loss of biodiversity is not considered a material risk for the Group".

Question 3: Scarcity of natural resources: "How do you foresee the scarcity of certain natural resources and the difficulties in supplying your strategic resources? How will it impact your business models and how will you secure your supply chains?"

Which companies stand out in the replies?

Certain groups have long since identified the scarcity of natural resources in their strategy and it is a focus area of strategy monitored at the highest level. As such, they have taken a head start on regulation—for example, in eco-design. However, for the most part, the subject is considered not part of the Corporate remit but of investment activity. The reply provided reduces the issue to a simple taxonomic definition. It is often difficult to find the right balance between simple compliance and a real commitment from the company.

Top best

For DANONE, a scarcity of resources has been identified in its strategy for some time, addressed with a much wider vision of responsibility, and supported for many years by tangible actions—as is also the case for SCHNEIDER. On their side, HERMES is developing a full approach, much like SAINT-GOBAIN, which has made the issue strategic.

Flops

AXA, the leading European insurance company, considers that the issue does not fall into the corporate remit, but its Asset Manager Investment activity. This leads to it bypassing the issue and this is worrying as a perspective given that there will be an increase in climate risks in the future to insure. PUBLICIS, which promotes green action in its clients advertising campaigns, seemingly does not apply these recommendations to itself. ORANGE mentions an interest on ecological matters, but via studies on rare earth elements when periods of scarcity of electronic components occur—and this narrow, purely economic angle, is regrettable.

How can the impact of the FIR's questions be increased?

Let's look at two areas of focus: potential proposals to improve the questions, and a more institutional approach that touches on the very ways and means to check the answers, and how the FIR could develop a strategy to increase its reach and influence.

Improving the impact of question 1

In 2021, the FIR was more precise in its demands than in 2020, with a concrete expectation of facts and data. However, our analysis considers several limits to the pertinence of the question such as it is currently formulated. In this light, the assessment criteria linked to the capex is not relevant to the service sector, notably financial services.

We believe that centring the assessment on capex, and how it is used, is limiting because the global environment in which these capex are used is also impactful in terms of CSR. Likewise, we noted that the optimisation of resources—including energy efficiency—is hardly more tackled than employee awareness, whereas these opex should be open to question, notably regarding R&D or HR costs for employee training, as indeed are the capex for growth. Finally, to mention the scope: scope 1/2/3 seems less subjective than that of the "value chain" to which it is referred to. In sum, we think that a segmentation of replies between the three major themes of decarbonisation, the use of resources, and biodiversity, is advisable.

Improving the impact of question 2

Loss of biodiversity does not have a tangible direct impact on corporate revenues—the deterioration of biodiversity generates scarcity in the stock of natural capital and causes damage to ecosystemic services.[8] It is a pity that the question addressed is negatively spun and only concerns the impact of the loss—and not the loss itself—of biodiversity, biodiversity conservation, and its re-growth. True, the regulations around biodiversity are not as mature as for other fields and this creates difficulty in assessing corporates' approaches and measuring the potential impact of these in limiting the loss, even protection of biodiversity. If we were to rephrase the question as such: "*Through your activities. . . . How do you limit the loss of biodiversity? How do you contribute to protecting biodiversity? Restore it? Specify the indicators, activities, geographical areas, and scope of your initiatives on the whole value chain*".

Improving the impact of question 3

Access to natural resources and the stakes in securing the supply chain is too often seen from an auto-centric and micro-economic angle. It corresponds to interpreting things in terms of risks (mapping, securing strategic suppliers, etc.) vis-à-vis production and company activity. Regrettably, there is no widening towards an ecosystem, nor a stakeholder approach. We even noted that tech companies equate scarcity of rare earth with scarcity of electronic components—whereas the current crisis in electronic components results from insufficient production capacity and the localisation of electronic components factories. All this has hardly a direct link with ecology.

Recommendations

Concerning the questions

The necessary continuity in timeframe to enable the one-year comparison between questions means confronting the risk of weariness linked to the repetition of the questions. Moreover, it overlooks the fact that the legal context or events—for example, the war in Ukraine—changes the stakes and could lead to prioritising the questions. Fairly open questions also lead to useful qualitative answers, but limit the possibility to make comparison. MCQs on certain topics, supplemented by qualitative comment sections could enable an improvement in the collected data. Also of interest would be to make a distinction between what stems from action required by norms, and good practice or proactive company initiatives.

Using a sector-by-sector approach is justified in that direct or indirect levers for action differ considerably from one to another, as well as the degree of maturity:

- Industrials: regroups industrial companies
- Metal and Mining
- Energy
- Construction and Building materials
- Consumer Goods and Retail
- Services: including financial (Bank Insurance).

Collecting information and the capacity to assess the reality of the announced policy

The link between the replies given to the FIR and the thematic sections of annual reports was duly checked in our work, even if it was at times a laborious undertaking. Indeed, it seemed important to us to differentiate the groups that have effective communication—and, as such, are well graded—but which are not necessarily the most virtuous at heart, and others who achieve concrete results but who are less able to present them.

Processing the replies

Regarding the replies: some companies refer directly to an "x or y page of an annual report"—an unsatisfactory practice in so much as the Reports have become voluminous. It is also important to identify who responds to the FIR's questions: the careful reading of replies shows very diverse degrees of pertinence and quality. Consequently, a preliminary question on the internal process that enables replies to be formulated and stakeholders identified (CSR, Comms, CEO, Board) is recommended. This equally facilitates the identification of the degree of engagement of senior management and the manner in which it is expressed. For example, Accor is correctly classified whereas S. Bazin in the HEC Alumni Mag argued that "true, we could do more, but look at how much we're moving while asking people not to wash their towels on a daily basis" (Coming from a CEO, should he really be saying that?). In an ideal world, the reply should also be able to identify if the company's ecosystem has been involved.

Modification of environmental questions for the 2022 General Assemblies
Question 1 **"You are explicitly committed to aligning your revenues and your investments (CAPEX/OPEX/R&D/mergers-acquisitions, etc.) with the Paris Agreement objective which aims at limiting global warming to 1.5 °C? How do you ensure that these revenues and investments meet this objective (please describe the methodologies used)? What are your main action plans and, as the case may be, the associated investment figures implemented to reach this objective in the short, medium, and long terms?"**

Question 2
"What percentage of your activities (expressed in turnover, net banking revenue, etc.) depends directly on biodiversity? What do you spend to support biodiversity?"
Question 3
"List the natural strategic resources required for the operation of your activity and/or that of your customers (water, energy, raw materials, etc.). How do you assess and calculate the impact of scarcity of resources on your business models? What initiatives do you set up to fight against difficulties of supply and seize opportunities to develop 'circular business models'? What are your objectives in this field?"

Towards a say on climate—and why not a say on biodiversity?

The increased importance of CSR in governance decisions is acknowledged. There is an increasingly demanding legal framework, as well as NGO activism which practices a "name and shame" approach and now attempts orchestrated trials by using the law—notably the duty of vigilance.[9] There is also the position of young generations concerning employer image, and the latter are joining the new influence held by engaged shareholders working to convince—or constrain—companies to progress towards CSR.

In that, the work of the FIR is pertinent and important and should broadly be able to be sustained. The approach of the FIR aiming to question the consensus, behind closed doors, of large corporations' boards is virtuous. This possibility for expression of minority shareholder engagement—sensitive to new stakes in CSR—is particularly beneficial. Highlighting this through the FIR's publications encourages companies to align themselves on best practices in terms of CSR and to choose the status of a mission-driven enterprise. It also goes hand in hand with other initiatives developed by several other actors, including the ESG firm Phitrust.

While the work so far carried out can be considered remarkable, the question of resources and means must be addressed. With the rise in ESG topics, and the means deployed by consulting firms such as ISS or Glass Lewis, FIR's work could be drowned out. Potential ways forward for the FIR are establishing their legitimacy by increasingly working with other stakeholders of the same vein and specialised in various fields; providing means to communicate to the wider public by working with media beyond the support of Novethic, the Caisse des Dépôts media branch dedicated to responsible finance; setting up a steering committee (equivalent to the governing committee of the Caisse des Dépôts) to gain support from expert trades, organisations or people who are figures of authority in their diverse fields. Moreover, gaining legitimacy in the role of activist and influencer are avenues to explore to give this concrete and positive initiative the role it could play in dialogue with investors, companies, and stakeholders, notably those from the ecology sphere.

As this chapter comes to an end, the 2022 General Assemblies have demonstrated throughout the world that strong questioning on a "say on climate" are emerging. In France, it is Terra Nova together with the FIR that first carried through this idea in April 2021 with the report *"Say on climate"—an urgent and pragmatic solution*. While companies still seem hesitant—three corporates put it on the agenda in 2020 (TotalEnergies, Vinci, and Atos) and four in 2022 (TotalEnergies, Carrefour, EDF, Engie)—ESG investors seem firmly decided to read it.

However, for this initiative to have an operational interest, several questions have to be raised. The first is that of the content—because the texts can vary enormously in terms of precision and engagement. As such, the FIR reproached TotalEnergies for a strategy that will impose the company "strong recourse to carbon offset" and considered that its investment projects are insufficient. The second question could be the periodicity of questioning: TotalEnergies has committed to do it every year due to the pressure exerted in 2020, 2021, and 2022, with a General Assembly disrupted by ecologist associations, but we are not sure it is efficient to do so, knowing that for any question of a strategic order a medium-term approach is required to assess the results and re-adjust? Finally, it can be noted that the resolutions obtained an 89% rate of approval—which is not bad. It could be doubly explained: the exercise is a complex one without standardised guidelines, thus shareholders give the benefit of the doubt to the CEO and her team, due to a lack of expertise. As time goes by, expertise increases and so do demands with pressure from NGOs and ESG funds.

As with any new strategic questioning of a company that queries the very heart of its business model, a certain amount of stammering is inevitable in the early phase. The positive questioning of the FIR, re-adjusted each year, enables the company—if it accepts to reply in good faith—fruitful dialogue with ESG analysts who themselves daily sharpen their practices on these vital issues.

Key takeaways:

- Companies with clear strategies, action plans, and specified capital expenditures (CAPEX) related to environmental goals tend to exhibit better practices and commitment to sustainability.
- Effective communication and transparency by companies regarding their environmental initiatives are essential for gaining shareholder support and improving their reputation.
- The expansion of environmental activism encompasses a diverse range of actors, including institutional investors, small shareholders, engaged proxies, and even NGOs.

Food for thought:

- To what extent should we ethically expect large companies to invest in sustainability initiatives? Why, then, do many large firms choose not to do so?

- The PACTE Law in France obliges companies to include a social and environmental mission dimension to its purpose (and included in the company statues). How should governments encourage CSR and sustainability practices? Through voluntarism or through legislation? Or both? Why?
- After reading the chapter, how do you feel about shareholder activism? To what extent do you think it effective? To what extent do you support more aggressive forms of activism?

Notes

1 de Beaufort, V. (2019, Juin). L'engagement actionnarial en France, vecteur de gouvernance pérenne? *Revue des sociétés*, n° 6.
2 Article 1833 of the Code civil: "The Company must be managed in its proper interest, while considering the social and environmental stakes of its activity."
3 www.phitrust.com/nous-connaitre/notre-approche-esg/.
4 Vérité 40 d'Axylia: www.axylia.com/v%C3%A9rit%C3%A940.
5 Rapport d'engagement 2020: www.frenchsif.org/isr-esg/publications/.
6 WP2202 CERESSEC: www.academia.edu/80055267/WP_2202_travaux_sur_le_questionnement_du_Forum_Pour_lInvestissement_Responsable.
7 A "Silent Spring" for the Financial System? Exploring Biodiversity-Related Financial Risks in France—August 2021, WP #826 Banque de France.
8 FINANCE & BIODIVERSITÉ COMPRENDRE ET AGIR: www.frenchsif.org/isr-esg/publications/.
9 Articles L.225–102–4 et L.225–102–5 du Code de commerce.

Part V

The energy transition

A focus on Asia and Africa

12 Geopolitical perspectives on China's sustainability initiatives

Cédomir Nestorovic

China's sustainability initiatives carry immense geopolitical implications. The whole world depends on China's efforts since the country emits twice the quantity of CO_2 than the second-ranked country, the United States. The task seems to be Sisyphean because China pursues two quasi-irreconcilable goals: on one side, it must implement green policies and on the other side it must sustain the growth of its economy.

There was a time before the Covid-19 pandemic when China was on track to achieve both goals but the Covid-19 lockdown and the economic problems resulting in lower GDP growth have forced the country to recalibrate its priorities. This recalibration has geopolitical consequences because China has the biggest manufacturing output in the world, it is the top trade partner for many countries in the world, and it is the world's main importer of natural resources. China is also the leading country for alternative sources of energy such as solar panels and electrical batteries. In sum, whatever China does, it will have an impact on other countries, hence the geopolitical importance of it.

This chapter delves into the geopolitical implications of China's sustainability initiatives. We will treat these implications from two points of view. The first one is classical geopolitics which puts emphasis on realism, facts, science, and a dichotomy between domestic policies and priorities versus international policies and priorities. This is especially important for sustainability initiatives because countries tend to prioritize their own interest before taking into account global interest. Classical geopolitics was, and still is, the dominant way of how geopolitics is viewed. The second is critical geopolitics which looks at geopolitics from a non-binary point of view—that is, with no domestic/international divide. It looks at politics and society from a social constructivism point of view and prioritizes knowledge over natural resources in the definition of power.[1] The non-binary approach is important because it treats the whole world as one system and looks at the environmental problems from the Anthropocene perspective.

DOI: 10.4324/9781003522355-17

Classical geopolitics' view on China's environmental initiatives

Classical geopolitics is the realm of facts, science, and realism on one side, and binary approach—domestic versus international divide—on the other. It fits well with the nature of the political system in which the Communist Party of China (CPC) plays the supreme role. CPC's insistence on science and technology comes from Marxism which puts emphasis on science and technology in improving the country's competitiveness and alleviating poverty.[2] Under the leadership of the CPC, China's investments in research and development, technological capabilities and innovation ecosystems have produced tremendous results. Not only has China succeed in eradicating extreme poverty in the country and ensured food security, but it has also become a world leader in AI, 5G telecommunications, e-commerce, and electric vehicles. All this happened in just 40 years, producing a tectonic shift in the balance of power in the 21st century and propelling China as the only challenger to the United States in the geopolitical arena.

This, however, comes with a price—and the price is environmental consequences, including air and water pollution, deforestation, and biodiversity loss. Because China embraced the proposal to be the factory of the world, China's greenhouse gas emissions have risen steadily, driven primarily by its reliance on coal for energy generation and heavy industries such as steel and cement production.

Despite significant investments in renewable energy and efforts to improve energy efficiency, China's absolute emissions continue to grow, making it the world's largest contributor to climate change. Among the greenhouse gases, Carbon dioxide (CO_2) is the most important one. Today, China is the biggest emitter of CO_2 in the world, with 11,336 million metric tons in 2021, while the United States is the second emitter with 5,032 million metric tons.[3] The third country, India, emitted half of the amount of US emissions, and one quarter of the Chinese emissions. Moreover, the primary source of CO_2 emissions in China is fossil fuels, most notably those that burn coal. About 58% of the total energy generated by China in 2021 came from coal alone.[4] China is by far the country with the highest coal generation (producing 6,631 Terawatt-hour -TWh, counting for 62% of electricity production) followed by India (947 TWh generated by coal, representing 71% of electricity production) and the United States (producing 774 TWh, and 19% of total electricity).[5] There is a huge difference between the three countries because from 2015 to 2020 India and the United States managed to decrease their dependence on coal while China did just the opposite. In addition, China is one of the biggest oil importers, which contributes to large CO_2 emissions.

Conscious about the environmental damage, China has put people's well-being front and centre, and implemented ambitious initiatives in fostering sustainability. On the political side, it set up the 2030 Agenda for Sustainable Development, built-up an inter-ministerial coordination mechanism made up of 45 ministries and agencies, and integrating its efforts with the country's

13th Five-Year Plan (2016–2020) which increased China's target for the use of non-fossil fuel energy sources to 15% over the period. It included wind energy and solar energy feed-in to the grid and prioritized dispatch policies for renewable energy.

The 14th Five-Year Plan (2020–2025) was prepared during the Covid-19 pandemic and a period of worsening relations between China and the United States. It put emphasis on internal problems such as future growth based on domestic consumption of goods and services and aimed to reduce disparities between urban and rural living standards. It did not forget its sustainability efforts though, since it announced goals for carbon neutrality by no later than 2060. Among the specific goals, half of the vehicles in China should be electric or fuel cell powered, and half hybrid by 2035. The Plan also forecasted achieving peak carbon emissions by the end of the 2020s and increasing the proportion of non-fossil fuel energy use to 20% by 2025, compared to 15% at the end of 2019. This will not be easy because the demand for electricity boosted demand for coal power in 2023, while the rebound from zero-Covid-19 boosted demand for oil.

China wants to reduce its dependence on coal and decrease overall pollution in large cities in the future by fostering the use of nuclear, renewable energy sources, and natural gas. But this will not happen overnight. The consumption of coal reached its highest ever level in 2023, so there is no reason to believe that the trend will decrease. China is still the biggest importer of coal (more than twice the amount imported by the second-ranked country, India) and since the biggest exporter of coal is Indonesia with 505.4 million tons (the second is Australia with 198 million tons), the global market looks like a bilateral monopoly with China as the importer and Indonesia as the supplier.[6] This differs from the oil market, which is much more diversified, with many buyers and sellers. China has a dominant position as a buyer for Indonesian and Australian coal and it can therefore transform this domination into a bargaining chip when it comes to political and security issues. This is especially true of China's relationship with Indonesia after restricting coal imports from Australia in 2019.[7]

The other element of classical geopolitics is a binary approach (domestic vs. international). China is a strong supporter of national sovereignty and clearly makes the difference between domestic and international realms. From the international point of view, China implements the Five Principles of Peaceful Coexistence: mutual respect for sovereignty and territorial integrity, mutual non-aggression, non-interference in each other's internal affairs, equality and mutual benefit, and peaceful coexistence. Even if these principles were formulated back in 1954, they are still valid today.[8] Mutual respect of sovereignty means that China will not accept that external forces impose something on China (including sustainability initiatives), and China will not try to impose something on other countries (including sustainability initiatives). All engagements by China and other countries in terms of ESG can only be voluntary.

When the Principles of Peaceful Coexistence were proposed by Zhou Enlai in 1954, China was just coming out of the Korean War and engaged in the preparation of the 1954 Sino-Indian Agreement. Today, China is powerful, and with great power comes great responsibility, not only for its own country and population, but also worldwide. In terms of sustainability initiatives, the most notable one is the green BRI, and its support of South-South cooperation. The Belt and Road Initiative launched in 2013 is the most ambitious project in decades. Its primary objective was economic cooperation, but in 2019, it was seconded by sustainability initiatives under the name of Belt and Road Initiative International Green Development Coalition (BRIGC or The Coalition).

The Coalition is an open, inclusive, and voluntary international network which brings together the environmental expertise of all partners included in the BRI to ensure that the Belt and Road brings long-term green and sustainable development to all concerned countries in support of the UN 2030 Agenda for Sustainable Development. The current set-up of the Coalition involves 134 partners, including 26 Environmental Ministries of UN Member States according to the United Nations.[9] The Coalition's mission is to integrate sustainable development, in particular environmental sustainability, international standards, and best practices, across the five priorities of the Belt and Road Initiative: policy coordination, infrastructure, trade, financial integration, and cultural exchanges. The goals are ambitious, but the results have yet to become significant. According to the Green Finance and Development Center (Fudan University, Shanghai), China's energy-related engagement in 2023 was the greenest in absolute and relative terms in any period since the BRI's inception, reaching US$7.9 billion. China has also increasingly invested in electricity transmission (over US$7 billion), metals and mining (+158%), which are particularly relevant to the green transition (e.g. lithium) and batteries for electric vehicles.[10] These are huge amounts, but they pale compared to the total investment in BRI, which have cumulatively reached more than US$1 trillion since its inception. The reason of relatively low commitments in sustainability initiatives comes from the fact that the main recipients of BRI investments are the developing countries in Africa, and countries in Africa must mitigate between poverty alleviation, food security and economic growth on one side—and green initiatives on the other. It is still possible to reconcile the two goals, as shown by the China–Ghana project on renewable energy launched in 2014 and funded by the Danish government. The project aims to implement off-grid community-based electrification, to increase the share of renewable energy and to promote the productive use of renewable energy on top of broader socio-economic and environmental objectives—most notably poverty reduction. The project has been highlighted by the United Nations Development Program as an example of successful South-South cooperation.[11]

Critical geopolitics' view on China's environmental initiatives

The second branch of geopolitics is critical geopolitics. It refers to a non-binary approach, social constructivism, and knowledge/power nexus. Following the non-binary postulate, critical geopolitics considers that sustainability efforts can only be effective if they are taken on a supra-national level because climate change and global warming do not know national boundaries.[12] Critical geopolitics in terms of space introduces a global and regional level of decision-making, and China has shown mixed results in that respect. China is an active participant in all global initiatives on sustainability. Not only does it actively participate in multilateral initiatives such as the UN SDG, the Paris Agreement, or the Convention on Biological Diversity, the country is also at the origin of specific proactive measures such as the Methane and Non-CO_2 Greenhouse Gases Summit at the UN Climate Change Conference (UNFCCC COP 28) in November 2023.

This initiative was co-sponsored by the United States, which shows that China and the United States can put their rivalry aside when the fate of the planet is concerned. China also initiated the Global Development Initiative in 2021 in order to promote the UN SDG goals.[13] As a result, more than 100 governments and international organizations have voiced support for GDI. From that point of view, China is clearly satisfying the critical geopolitics criteria. However, its insistence on national sovereignty and voluntary commitment to sustainability goals casts a shadow on its effectiveness, especially when the relationships with its immediate neighbours do not show the same consistency. Two important possibilities of cooperation exist. The first is the proposal of a 'shared Himalaya'.[14] The Hindu Kush Himalayan region is the location of several of Asia's great river systems which provide water for drinking, irrigation, and other uses for about 1.5 billion people, and the two biggest countries—China and India—cannot find an agreement on it. The second is the agreement on the Mekong River. Such an agreement would enable the number of dams located on Chinese upstream side of the river to be limited.[15] For the moment, China is not part of the Mekong River Commission. It appears that it is easier for China to reach an agreement with its far away archrival the United States, rather than with its neighbours India, Vietnam, or Laos.

As far as social constructivism is concerned, critical geopolitics insists on the fact that society can change the definition of everything, including the state or sustainability. The society or political leaders can declare that sustainability goals have been achieved just by changing the criteria. For example, there used to be 'Potemkin villages' in Tsarist Russia when fake constructions or facades were built to make people believe that the situation was better that it was. In the case of sustainability, one country could challenge the very existence of ecological problems, global warming, climate change and the human contribution to these problems. A country could also give false figures or give no figures at all about their achievements in pursuing sustainability goals.

This is not what China is doing. It does not pursue conspiracy theories, and does not question human contribution to global ecological problems. The lack of information disclosure was observed by the WHO during the Covid-19 pandemic, but when it comes to sustainability efforts, there is no suspicion of non-cooperation. If some information is indeed falsified, it usually comes from local authorities which want to outsmart Beijing's instructions, rather than from the central government itself.[16]

Finally, for the knowledge-power nexus, critical geopolitics puts the emphasis on the nature of knowledge that is produced, who is producing it and what the objective of producing a specific knowledge is. In the case of China, the country has adopted the same standards as in the other countries. Its specificity lies in solutions. Indeed, what kind of solution-based knowledge is pursued is the main concern.[17] Among the huge variety of renewable energy solutions, China has opted for two of them: photovoltaic technologies and electric batteries. Not only is China the biggest producer of technology, it is also the leader in patent filing for renewable energies. Sustainable energy includes renewable energy sources such as wind and solar, energy storage, efficiency, grid management, and electric transport. According to the IRENA (International Renewable Energy Agency)—INSPIRE (International Standards and Patents in Renewable Energy) Platform, China has filed more than 48,000 patents in 2021, while the second-best country, the United States, has filed only 6,950 patents.[18] There is an ongoing debate about the quality of patents filed by China, but the country pursues the adage 'from quantity, will come quality'. The combination of a huge research activity and industry readiness to apply that research gives China an undisputed leadership in the production of green technologies. Because of its specific political system, China is probably the only country in the world that can enrol state-owned enterprises and private companies in supporting its initiative such as the 'Made in China 2025' plan to promote high-tech manufacturing and the development of green technologies.

Towards the future

Both branches of geopolitics—classical and critical geopolitics—recognize that no sustainable effort on a global scale can succeed without active Chinese participation. China is the biggest emitter of greenhouse gases in the world and at the same time the biggest purveyor of research—in terms of patent files—and production of renewable energy technology and solutions. It is therefore of paramount importance that Chinese sustainable initiatives succeed.

There is no doubt about Chinese sincerity in pursuing sustainability initiatives launched either by the international community or by China itself, but China has also to cope with domestic economic problems and sanctions initiated by the United States and other Western countries. If China succeeds in combining economic growth and green initiatives, the whole world will benefit from it. Moreover, at the same time it would be a significant contribution to its soft power and leadership in South-South relationships.

Key takeaways:

- China's sustainability initiatives carry immense geopolitical implications. China is also the leading country for alternative sources of energy such as solar panels and electrical batteries.
- Under the leadership of the CPC, China has succeed in eradicating extreme poverty and ensured food security, and become a world leader in AI, 5G telecommunications, e-commerce, and electric vehicles.
- The price is environmental consequences, including air and water pollution, deforestation, and biodiversity loss. China's greenhouse gas emissions have risen steadily, driven primarily by its reliance on coal for energy generation and heavy industries such as steel and cement production.
- The 14th Five-Year Plan (2020–2025) announced goals for carbon neutrality by no later than 2060. Half of the vehicles in China should be electric or fuel cell powered, and half hybrid by 2035.
- China wants to reduce its dependence on coal and decrease overall pollution in large cities in the future by fostering the use of nuclear, renewable energy sources, and natural gas.
- China has a dominant position as a buyer for Indonesian and Australian coal and it can therefore transform this domination into a bargaining chip when it comes to political and security issues.
- China implements the Five Principles of Peaceful Coexistence: mutual respect for sovereignty and territorial integrity, mutual non-aggression, non-interference in each other's internal affairs, equality and mutual benefit, and peaceful coexistence.
- All engagements by China and other countries in terms of ESG can only be voluntary.
- Notable sustainability initiatives include the Belt and Road Initiative International Green Development Coalition (BRIGC or The Coalition).
- China is an active participant in all global initiatives on sustainability and at the origin of specific proactive measures, for example the 2021 Global Development Initiative in order to promote the UN SDG goals. More than 100 governments and international organizations have voiced support for GDI.
- But two areas of cooperation remain frozen: 'shared Himalaya'. Proposal and agreement on the Mekong River.
- China's specificity lies in solutions: China has opted for photovoltaic technologies and electric batteries. China is the biggest producer of technology and also the leader in patent filing for renewable energies.
- China is probably the only country in the world that can enrol state-owned enterprises and private companies in supporting its initiative.

Food for thought:

- Think of your perceptions of China before reading this chapter and your perceptions now. How have they changed? And to what extent have you gained insights into China's standpoint on sustainability?

- This chapter mentioned the Belt and Road Initiative International Green Development Coalition. What effect will that have on your country in terms of economic impact, sustainability impact, and geopolitical impact?
- And to what extent will—once the BRIGC is completed—this initiative change the world?

Notes

1 The difference between classical and critical geopolitics is given in Nestorovic, C. (2023). *Geopolitics and business, relevance and resonance*. Springer.
2 Chen, H., & Su, R. (2023). The Marxist view of science and technology and China's independent innovation and development. *Journal of Education and Educational Research*, 4(2), 73–77.
3 Results for 2021 available at https://globalcarbonatlas.org/emissions/carbon-emissions.
4 www.eia.gov/international/analysis/country/CHN.
5 www.ember-climate.org/insights/research/top-25-coal-power-countries-in-2020.
6 Maguire, G. (2024, January 18). Global coal exports and power generation hit new highs in 2023. *Reuters*.
7 Manullang, G. H., & Isnarti, R. (2023). China's energy diplomacy to coal imports from Indonesia after restricting coal import from Australia in 2019. *Indonesian Journal of Energy*, 6(2), 72–85.
8 Speech by Assistant Foreign Minister Miao Deyu attending the Forum on Developing Countries and International Law and the Seminar Commemorating the 70th Anniversary of the Five Principles of Peaceful Coexistence, April 24, 2024. www.fmprc.gov.cn/eng/wjbxw/202404/t20240425_11289117.html.
9 www.unep.org/regions/asia-and-pacific/regional-initiatives/belt-and-road-initiative-international-green.
10 Wang, C. N. *China Belt and Road Initiative (BRI) investment report 2023*. https://greenfdc.org/china-belt-and-road-initiative-bri-investment-report-2023/.
11 *China-Ghana South-South Cooperation on Renewable Energy Technology Transfer*. www.undp.org/china/projects/china-ghana-south-south-cooperation-renewable-energy-technology-transfer.
12 See Dalby, S. (2020). *Anthropocene geopolitics, globalization, security, sustainability*. University of Ottawa Press.
13 Wu, L. (2023, July 11). China's transition from the belt and road to the global development initiative. *The Conversation*.
14 Goodale, E., Mammides, C., Mtemi, W., Chen, Y. F., Barthakur, R., Goodale, U. M., Jiang, A., Liu, J., Malhotra, S., Meegaskumbura, M., & Pandit, M. K. (2022). Increasing collaboration between China and India in the environmental sciences to foster global sustainability. *Ambio*, *51*, 1474–1484.
15 Osborne, M. (2022, April 12). How the Mekong River Commission ignores reality. *Lowy Institute*. www.lowyinstitute.org/the-interpreter/how-mekong-river-commission-ignores-reality.
16 Xie, E. (2019, May 19). China's green efforts hit by fake data and corruption among the grass roots. *South China Morning Post*.
17 For knowledge production and environmental problems, see O'Lear, S. (2018). *Environmental geopolitics*. Rowman and Littlefield.
18 https://inspire.irena.org/Pages/patents/Patents-Search.aspx.

13 Why and how Morocco is pioneering Africa's energy transition?

Hugues Bouthinon-Dumas and Hamid Bouchikhi

Morocco is often cited as an example of renewable energy policy. The gigantic solar power plants occupying hundreds of hectares of desert in the Ouarzazate region have become an iconic image of the energy transition in developing countries and particularly in Africa. These spectacular pictures are promoted not only by the Moroccan authorities but also by numerous institutions engaged in ecological transition around the world. They are intended to illustrate the virtues of political voluntarism in responding to the contemporary ecological crisis. Global warming due to greenhouse gas emissions makes it urgent to dramatically reduce reliance on fossil fuels in favour of decarbonized and renewable energies.

The development of renewable energies is viewed not only as a major achievement for Morocco but also as an initiative that could lead the energy transition in the rest of Africa. While Moroccan officials, international finance organizations, and specialized consulting firms assert that Morocco's energy strategy paves the way for Africa's ecological transition, the evidence of success is preliminary and the time is ripe for a critical review of the strategy.

In this chapter, we examine the implementation and evolution of a national strategy launched at the end of the 2000s. To do so, we will draw on various official and independent sources, including the report published by the Moroccan Economic, Social and Environmental Council (CESE) in 2019 and the general report published, in 2021, by the Special Commission on the New Development Model (CSMD).[1]

What were the motivations of the strategy and the problems it sought to solve? How effectively has Morocco executed the strategy over the last 15 years? To what extent is the development of renewable energies likely to contribute to socio-economic development and to the ecological transition in Morocco and, more generally, in Africa?

In the first section, we will look at the genesis of Morocco's bold energy transition strategy and discuss the respective weights, in its inception, of self-interest versus principled commitment to the fighting of global warming. In the second section, we summarize the regulatory, financial, and organizational architecture set up to support the execution of the strategy. In the third section, we review the achievements, so far, of the strategy. In the

DOI: 10.4324/9781003522355-18

fourth and last section, we share reflections on the future of Morocco's energy transition.

The origins of Morocco's energy transition

The massive construction, in Morocco, of electricity generation capacity using renewable energy sources, particularly solar and wind power, is anything but the product of spontaneous market forces. Rather, it is the consequence of public policy and a proactive commitment on the part of the Moroccan authorities. What were, then, the reasons behind the strategy and who are the people driving its formulation and execution?

The rationale for the strategy: a mix of self-interest and environmental activism

The development of renewable energies from 2009—for solar power—to 2010—for wind power—stems from three categories of reasons. Morocco's commitment to invest massively in renewable energies was, first and foremost, driven by the need to reduce its dependence on imported hydrocarbons. As the country's subsoil is poor in fossil fuels—at least in view of the explorations carried out to date—the country had to import 97% of its energy mix in 2012. Standing at 90% in 2023, the energy bill weighed, and still weighs, heavily on the country's trade balance (21% of imports in 2022) and on its balance of payments. Moreover, this burden is, on the one hand, compounded by the high level of volatility of gas and oil prices, and on the other the volatility of the exchange rates on the other.

When Morocco decided to prioritize renewable energies as a substitute for fossil fuels, it also emphasized the natural advantages of the country's geographical location. Morocco has abundant and regular wind energy resources, both at sea on the Atlantic coast and on land in the north of the country. Solar resources are also exceptional, as the number of sunny days is particularly high. Renewable energy plants can be set up in desert or offshore areas, which have hardly been exploited until now.

Lastly, Morocco justifies the development of renewable energies with arguments linked to the ecological transition and the need to fight climate change, which is hitting African countries particularly hard. This argument has been played out from the beginning of the energy transition policy and has gained in importance as the issue moved to the heart of the global agenda. Morocco's activism was instrumental in the United Nations decision to organize the 1996 high profile COP 22 meeting in Marrakech. For ten days, Morocco was at the centre of a global conversation and could claim the role of an exemplary country committed to the ecological transition starting with energy.

So, in a sort of clever move, Morocco is solving its high dependence on fossil fuels by leveraging its geography and presenting its strategy, to the rest of the world, as a commitment to fighting global warming. Mixing self-interest with benevolence enables the country in its discussions with international finance organizations whose contributions are essential to fund the execution of the energy transition strategy.

The role of political will in the formulation of the strategy

Morocco embarked very early on the construction of renewable energy power plants. While this policy may seem obvious today, as many countries are moving in this direction to achieve the carbon neutrality required by the Paris Agreement, it is important to emphasize that when Morocco committed to renewable energy, the strategy was a wager. At that time, energy production costs from renewable sources were much higher than they are today, and the profitability of projects highly uncertain.

While Morocco's dependence on fossil fuels was an important factor, it alone did not determine the country's energy transition strategy (Vermeren, 2009/2011). The strategy was, and continues to be, driven at the highest level of the state, by King Mohamed VI who emphasized the agenda in several public statements starting with the royal speech of 30 July 2008 where he laid, for the first time, the foundations for the energy transition strategy.

> This also applies to the challenges that Morocco faces in terms of energy. Indeed, it is now up to us to adapt to the profound changes affecting this sector on a global scale, and which everything suggests will not fade away, but rather get worse and worse. It is therefore necessary to follow a policy combining, on the one hand, the rational management of energy products and, on the other hand, the adoption of an efficient strategy aimed at reducing energy consumption, without harming productivity. It is also necessary to ensure, as part of this approach, the protection and diversification of energy sources. Morocco has no choice but to strengthen its local energy production capacity and pave the way for promising investments in energy supply. It must also resolutely pursue efforts aimed at making alternative and renewable energies the keystone of national energy policy.[2]

The King set a highly ambitious target of 52% of renewables in the electricity mix by 2030, up from 32% in 2009. Thanks to his personal interest and supervision, the energy strategy enjoys the status of a "regalian policy" which places it high on the domestic policy agenda and insulates it from bureaucratic inertia and changing governments. Following on the impetus provided by the King, governments articulated an ambitious "National Energy Strategy" and passed specific legislation, such as Law 13–09 which modifies the legal framework for energy production and distribution to enable the development of renewable energy projects.

To drive implementation, the King oversaw the creation, in 2010, of the Moroccan Agency for Solar Energy (MASEN), a public, legally autonomous organization dedicated to the design, construction, and operation of solar power plants. To execute its mission, MASEN is authorized to borrow from international lenders and sells its output to the national electricity utility (ONEE) according to predetermined tariffs. Later, in 2016, MASEN's mandate was extended to all forms of renewable energies. Its acronym stands, now, for "Moroccan Agency for Sustainable Energy".

On the people side of the process, execution is driven by a small group of carefully chosen "technocrats" who occupy key positions at MASEN and other parts of the emerging renewable energies ecosystem. They are empowered and accountable to the King who chairs periodic reviews of the strategy.

State-driven initiatives, regulations, and projects have created a favourable environment for domestic and foreign investments in renewable energy projects. The involvement of the royal holding Al Mada in renewable energies, through Nareva, a specialized subsidiary, gives confidence to other investors in the strategy.

The deployment of energy transition projects in Morocco

Morocco's energy transition strategy has materialized in a number of physical infrastructure projects. These projects are enabled by legal and financial arrangements that are reviewed in this section.

A series of projects in operating and planning stages

Renewable energy power plants were launched at the end of the 2000s and have gradually come online since the 2010s. Some plants are under construction while other projects are still in the planning stage.

In fact, Morocco's energy transition goes back further than that. Morocco has a large number of hydroelectric power stations, built during the reign of King Hassan II. They still produce a significant proportion of Morocco's carbon-free energy, although it is not these 148 dams that are attracting the most attention.

The projects that have been completed, or are under construction, consist of large-scale solar plants or wind farms. Several gigantic solar power plants—Noor Ouarzazate 1, 2, 3, for example—using different technologies, have been built in the desert region of Ouarzazate. In addition, wind farms have been built both on land, notably in the Tangiers region, and at sea to harness the winds off Morocco's Atlantic coast.

These constructions are spectacular, as portions of the desert are covered with mirrors or photovoltaic panels, and numerous wind turbine masts rise out of the ocean.

The legal and financial arrangements that enabled these projects to come to fruition

The deployment of solar and wind power plants is not only a technical success in terms of engineering and technology, it is also a success based on the legal and financial arrangements that have made these mega investments possible.

The various renewable energy installations are not based on the same types of structures, as the wind power sector is based on private projects, while solar power plant projects are the result of private–public partnerships. Although the Moroccan authorities are very keen to develop this energy industry, the power plants are not produced and operated by public entities. Power plant construction projects are the subject of calls for tender to which various financial and industrial players can respond within the framework of consortia. The financial resources needed for these capital-intensive projects are raised by MASEN, which then passes them on to the companies selected to develop the projects. The energy production sites are built by companies from various countries, including Spain and China, to name but two, with Moroccan companies also participating, notably through subcontracting. The energy produced by these plants is then purchased by the National Office of Electricity and Drinking Water (ONEE), the public utility, on the basis of long-term contracts (PPA) that secure the supply of electricity and the income of the operating companies.

The construction of power plants falls into the category of infrastructure projects, which are also part of a developing country's ecological transition. These projects can therefore benefit from special financing—development aid, funds investing in long-term projects—from private, international or semi-public lenders, including EIB, AFD, KfW, to name but several. The growing appetite of certain investors for projects typical of the ecological transition is also enabling Morocco to raise funds in the form of green bonds, for example. For its energy transition, the Kingdom of Morocco has thus been able to take advantage of international funding sources and was not constrained by the dearth of domestic financial resources.

The renewable energy power plants built in Morocco over the last 15 years represent a political, legal, and financial achievement, as well as an industrial and technical one. However, the fact that these plants are up and running does not mean that the policy has been a total success.

An assessment of Morocco's energy transition policy

To determine whether Morocco's energy transition policy has been a success, we need to assess the ability of existing and future projects to solve the problems that prompted the policy in the first place. From this point of view, the results are mixed: while renewable energy production capacity is impressive, it remains below the initial target and has generated a high level of debt. Moreover, Morocco's energy policy remains ambiguous insofar as the country has not given up on the exploration of fossil fuels reserves.

Tangible results, but below initial targets

Morocco's energy policy has resulted in a very significant increase in renewable electricity generation capacity—2277 MGW in 2021 compared to 2009. However, the initial target of 42% renewables in the electricity mix by 2020 was missed. The new target stands at 52% by 2030. In 2021, renewable sources, including hydroelectric plants, represented about 37% versus 32% in 2009. It is important to underline that total electricity consumption grew by 78% between 2009 and 2021. A nuanced reading of these figures would suggest a relative success of the strategy. Without investments in local production, through solar and wind plants, the increase in electricity consumption could have aggravated the country's dependence on imported fossil fuels.

Morocco had also set itself the goal of diversifying its energy sources, with wind, solar power, and hydropower each accounting for a third of the renewable energies produced. In practice, wind power has developed more rapidly than solar power—1,466 versus 811 MGW in 2021—while hydroelectric output remains constant over the years, standing at 1,760 MGW. Interestingly, Morocco communicates massively on solar power plants and this focus explains the country's excellent ranking in the Climate Change Performance Index and international recognition.

However, Morocco's achievements in wind and solar cannot obscure the fact that the goal of independence from fossil fuels is far from being achieved. The rate of dependence was still around 90% in 2021. As said earlier, this is due to the country's increased demand for energy. Demographic growth, population affluence, rural exodus and the development of energy-intensive industrial activities have all led to a significant increase in energy consumption, up 78% in 2021 compared to 2009.

Morocco's energy strategy has also led to high public indebtedness, since it is public entities that largely bear the economic risk resulting from technological choices that are now being called into question. MASEN initially chose to develop solar power plants using molten salt (CSP) or tower technology, rather than photovoltaic panels. As the public energy utility, ONEE, is compelled by law to buy the electricity produced by MASEN, the first power plants in service—Noor 1 and Noor 2 in particular—are generating a high financial burden. Together, MASEN and ONEE are responsible for 35% of public indebtedness, not including borrowing by the treasury department. The CESE report points out that Morocco's energy policy ultimately affects the country's credit rating and thus limits the investments the country could need to fund ecological transition.

Morocco's energy transition policy is also disappointing in other respects. In particular, the CESE notes that favouring mega solar plants and wind farms, at the expense of decentralized solutions, is a capital-intensive proposition and creates few jobs. Local industrial integration, another goal of the strategy, has been very modest. There are few Moroccan subcontractors for specific components in the wind and solar energy sectors, and some have even encountered difficulties that have led to the closure of production sites such as the Siemens-Gomesa wind turbine blade factory near Tangiers.

Only a partial conversion to renewable energy

Morocco's energy transition to renewable energies does not mean the country's complete conversion to decarbonized, environmentally friendly modes of energy production. The continuation or even intensification of hydrocarbon-related activities shows that Morocco has not really given up fossil fuels and turned definitively to clean energies, as is often claimed. Indeed, several facts show that Morocco has not completely turned its back on fossil fuels:

- Morocco continues to hope to discover fossil energy resources underground. The National Office for Hydrocarbons and Mines (ONHYM) has not stopped prospecting for hydrocarbons.
- Over the period 2010–2024, Morocco made major investments in the port storage of hydrocarbons.
- Some very costly infrastructures concern the hydrocarbon industry, such as the Nigeria-Morocco gas pipeline project.
- The most polluting fossil fuels, such as coal, continue to play an important role in Morocco's energy mix (e.g. the Safi power plant).
- At individual level too, fossil fuels continue to be used massively by the population, as the government continues to subsidise butane consumption by households and businesses alike.

Aside from the bold strategic intent and the development of gigantic wind and solar power plants and farms, Morocco's energy transition is a work in progress, insofar as renewables are still far from the target for 2030 and the country continues to rely heavily on fossil fuels.

Prospects for Morocco's energy transition

In light of the facts, it would appear that the often-heard claim that Morocco has resolutely embarked on the ecological transition—thanks to a proactive policy aimed at substituting renewable energies for fossil fuels—needs to be qualified. The efforts made in the wind and solar power sectors are just the beginning. It is time for Morocco to complete its ecological transition strategy, which is essentially limited to renewable energies. The country needs to make crucial choices for the future.

Integrating energy policy into a broader model of sustainable development

The policy of promoting renewable energies is only one component of the energy transition. Although the quest for energy efficiency and sobriety were stated objectives from the launch of the energy transition policy in the late 2000s, it is essentially in the field of wind and solar energy that Morocco has been successful. And even beyond energy policy, it seems crucial that Morocco initiate a broader policy of ecological and social transition to resolve the various challenges and crises of global warming, water stress, inclusive economic development, and still others (Bouvier, 2021). Morocco's lead in developing renewable energies contrasts with its lag in other aspects of sustainable development such as water management (Mehdi Falloul, 2015), waste management and recycling, pollution control and environmental protection, access to healthcare, and improving the quality of education. The construction of wind and solar power plants appears to be a technical and, to a lesser extent, an economic success which lacks connection with broader, sustainable, social, and economic development.

Top Moroccan officials are aware of the need to extend the ecological transition policy beyond the energy transition (Commission spéciale sur le Modèle de Développement, 2021). Part of the King's speech on the occasion of his 24-year reign was devoted to this subject, showing that this concern is taken into account at the highest level. The CESE report (2019, 2020) stresses that Morocco's new energy policy must become a lever for more substantial transformation of the Moroccan economy. Energy policy must be conceived as a trigger for "new green economic growth". The industrial spin-offs of energy policy and synergies between economic sectors must be sought as part of Morocco's new structural economic policy. According to the CESE, the separate development of different initiatives and policies (silos) must come to an end. Some initiatives, such as the "EnR cluster", are good steps towards the creation of ecosystems which can enable different players to benefit together from a new generation of investments in the energy of the future.

The need to update Morocco's energy strategy

Morocco embarked on the path of renewable energies with determination and before many other countries. The strategy was ambitious and pioneering. However, this policy was not defined once and for all and has been revised several times.

Morocco presents green hydrogen (Power-to-X) as the core of its new energy policy. Hydrogen produced from decarbonized energy represents a step beyond renewable energies. It is presented as a major new axis of Morocco's energy policy.

The CESE draws up a precise diagnosis of the various adjustments to the current policy that need to be made at different levels, including regulation and governance. It also sets out new ambitions for Moroccan energy production. This should enable the decarbonization of transport and the pursuit of the country's industrial development, particularly in economic development zones such as Tangiers.

In fact, these ambitions appear to be too many. Even if Morocco continues to invest in the construction of new renewable energy production capacity, it will not be possible to satisfy the many components of domestic demand at the same time as selling electricity to Europe. New decarbonized power generation capacity is expected on all sides:

- to enable households and businesses to benefit from low-cost energy (whereas prices did not fall since projects were launched in the 2000s);
- to desalinate seawater to compensate for water deficits;
- to enable the production of green hydrogen, which could then be used locally or exported, notably to Europe;
- to develop promising industrial sectors such as worm fertilizers and ammonia;
- for use by energy-intensive industries exporting products to Europe.

One of the challenges of clean electricity is that Morocco should not be hampered by the ecological regulations that the European Union is setting up, such as the Carbon Border Adjustment Mechanism (CBAM). Part of Morocco's attractiveness, particularly for industrial groups in industries such as automotive and aeronautics, lies in the fact that it can manufacture equipment or assemble products under conditions that are deemed acceptable by European authorities, who are increasingly concerned not to import products with a high carbon footprint.

It is easy to understand why Morocco's success in renewable energies gives rise to numerous ideas for using this clean energy! However, it is unrealistic to think that it will be possible to go in all these directions simultaneously. Even if Morocco stays on its high trajectory of investment in renewable energies, the amount of energy that can be produced will remain limited. Moreover, it will be partly absorbed by demographic growth and the expected rise in the population's average standard of living. Morocco will therefore have limited room for manoeuvre. Faced with the multitude of uses envisaged for the additional electricity that could be produced, choices will necessarily have to be made. And these choices will be at the heart of the new energy policy that Morocco must define today.

This is not to say that Morocco's spectacular success in building renewable energy plants will not contribute to Africa's ecological transition. We simply have to recognize that the effect of Morocco's energy transition on Africa's ecological transition will not be direct. Above all, it is by pioneering an energy transition policy that Morocco will be able to inspire other African countries.

The Xlinks project echoes the DESERTEC project developed by German engineers linked to the German branch of the Club of Rome in the early 2000s. They imagined producing electricity from the immense solar resources in North Africa and exporting it to Europe. Xlinks' aim is to transmit electricity generated from renewable energy sources in Morocco to south-west England via 3,800 km of very high voltage cables. If the project comes to fruition, it will mean that Morocco's energy policy includes a strong component of production for export.

Key takeaways:

- Morocco is cited as an example of renewable energy policy: it a major achievement for Morocco and an initiative that could inspire the energy transition in the rest of Africa.
- The massive construction of electricity generation capacity using renewable energy sources is the consequence of public policy and a proactive commitment on the part of the Moroccan authorities.
- The strategy is driven at the highest level of the state by King Mohamed VI. This is manifested in the 2010 creation of the Moroccan Agency for Solar Energy (MASEN), a public, legally autonomous organization authorized to borrow from international lenders and selling its output to the national electricity utility ONEE.
- It has also seen the construction of infrastructure projects: Renewable energy power plants, large-scale solar plants or wind farms, etc.
- The construction of power plants benefits from special financing—development aid, funds investing in long-term projects—from private, international or semi-public lenders.
- While renewable energy production capacity is impressive, it remains below the initial target and has generated a high level of debt. Morocco's energy policy remains ambiguous: the country has not given up on the exploration of fossil fuels reserves.
- Beyond energy policy, it is crucial for Morocco to initiate a broader policy of ecological and social transition to resolve the various challenges and crises of global warming, water stress, inclusive economic development.
- There is a need to update Morocco's energy strategy to render it capable of satisfying domestic demand and selling electricity to Europe.
- It is by pioneering an energy transition policy that Morocco will be able to inspire other African countries.

Food for thought:

- Compared to the success of Morocco's development of renewable energy sources, how does your country fare? Why is that?
- To what extent do countries with a centralized system of power and authority have the advantage over "looser", more pluralistic countries in getting things done? Is there a "half-way" house lesson to learn and what is that in detail?
- How do you see Morocco developing in the next 20 to 30 years? What do you think will be its weight on the international scene and in terms of reaching the UN SDGs?

Notes

1 The second author was a member of the Special Commission on the Development Model (CSMD) appointed by King Mohammed VI to review of the country's development trajectory and recommend a new development model.
2 Authors' translation assisted by Google Translate.

References

Bouvier, M. (Dir.). (2021). *Financement de la santé et de l'éducation dans un monde en mutation. Quelles approches au Maroc et en France?* LGDJ.

Commission spéciale sur le Modèle de Développement. (2021, avril). *Le nouveau modèle de développement. Libérer les énergies et restaurer la confiance pour accélérer la marche vers le progrès et la prospérité pour tous.* Rapport général.

Conseil économique social et environnemental (CESE). (2019). *Le Nouveau Modèle de Développement du Maroc.* https://www.csmd.ma/documents/Rapport_General.pdf

Conseil économique social et environnemental (CESE). (2020). *Accélérer la transition énergétique pour installer le Maroc dans la croissance verte.* Avis n°45.

Mehdi Falloul, M. E. (2015). *Economie et gestion de l'eau au Maroc.* Edilivre.

Vermeren, P. (2009/2011). *Le Maroc de Mohammed VI: la transition inachevée.* La découverte.

Conclusion: Implications for business schools

The current environmental situation calls for a profound questioning of what is taught, researched, and done in business schools. Business schools have been traditionally focusing on the social sciences—for example, economics, sociology, psychology—to understand, and teach, how organizations operate and relate with society and the economy. In the Anthropocene, the need for ecological transformation requires business schools to open up to other domains that do not belong to the social sciences but relate to the natural environment.[1] Engaging with the natural environment implies learning not only about greenhouse gas emissions and the specificities of climate change, but also about other urgent issues such as water management or biodiversity collapse. These different biophysical dimensions are captured by the nine "planetary boundaries" identified by the Stockholm Resilience Center.[2] These boundaries are limits beyond which the earth may not be able to self-regulate and maintain a safe and sustainable environment for humanity. Research has shown that most of those limits have been crossed, pointing to the unsustainable nature of business-as-usual that led to this situation.[3] Integrating these aspects in the curriculum necessitates engaging with other faculties such as the physics, biology, or chemistry departments, which have very different perspectives from what is currently taught in business schools.

The current situation also calls for business schools to question the drivers of development and prosperity of companies over the last decades, namely globalization and digitalization. Globalization has had a dramatic impact on the increase of CO_2 emissions.[4] The impact of digitalization on carbon emissions is more ambiguous as the carbon intensity per use is reducing, while carbon emission per capita is increasing due to the development of new uses.[5] Nevertheless, the current development of new technologies is likely to have a significant impact on the Anthropocene. The International Energy Agency[6] forecast that demand for electricity is likely to double worldwide between 2024 and 2026 due to crypto currencies and artificial intelligence.

The ecological crisis also goads us to reconsider how we think about innovation. Innovation is often associated with resorting to new technologies to disrupt established competitive positions and generate more profit regardless of the environmental impact. In the Anthropocene, we need to take into account the ecological footprint of innovations as well. Technology can play a major role in finding efficient ways to produce and use electricity, or in developing new technologies of carbon capture, use and storage (CCUS) that is necessary to achieve a net zero economy. It also calls for promoting a more open-minded approach to innovation that is not restricted to adding more technology but adopting low-tech solutions, frugal innovations, and traditional knowledge to develop low carbon solutions.

In the Anthropocene, business schools must anticipate and reflect on the evolution of the economic context in which companies operate. Over the last decades, business schools have made significant contributions to economic growth by training entrepreneurs and incubating start-ups. New businesses are deemed "successful" when they have higher turnover, profit, geographical coverage and valuation. From this perspective, rapid growth, or "hypergrowth", was celebrated as a goal in itself, rather than a means. However, growth in the Anthropocene also corresponds to an exhaustion of natural resources. Moreover, increasing regulation to limit negative externalities such as carbon emissions is likely to compromise companies that depend on the extraction or use of massive quantities of resources, as well as business models whose growth implies more negative externalities. It also brings into question notions of hypergrowth and prepares future entrepreneurs and business executives for a context of limited growth or degrowth. Consequently, a revision of the definition of success is due: is it about expansion, or resilience and the capacity to operate and thrive in an increasingly uncertain environment.

Business schools can draw from recent developments in circular economy, rethinking business models and teaching new ways of assessing them. While companies are now aware of the need to integrate non-financial dimensions as key aspects of their activities a lot remains to be done to develop business models that combine economic activity with a sustainable impact on the environment. It is probably too early to decide whether emerging approaches such as "regenerative companies"[7] are promising new directions to build sustainable business models, or mere buzzwords to justify consultants' fees. The integration of environmental and social dimensions to the traditional financial dimensions[8] radically questions how value is defined, what the "real" costs of production are, and how profit can be made once social and environmental costs are included. While start-up and scale-up companies are integrating the non-financial aspects in their purpose and business plan, more remains to be done by mature companies. They need to question their existing practices, revise their models and portfolio of activities, lower their carbon footprint, and exploit the new opportunities that emerge from the Anthropocene.

The challenge is huge for business schools. They must educate students as well as executives to help them transition towards more sustainable business models. The ecological crisis questions what business schools teach, the promises they make to students, and the aspirations they fulfil. Most "business schools" do not teach how to do "business" but how to "manage".[9] Whereas "business" suggests a sole focus on for-profit activities, these schools offer a much broader education and teach students how to "manage" organizations regardless of whether they are profitable or not. This broader perspective is likely to be especially useful in uncertain times where resilience might imply being able to envision solutions beyond immediate financial return. The capacity to develop long-term thinking rather than focusing on short-term profit maximization is typically something that business schools can teach.

As mentioned before, the changing context questions the traditional emphasis on the social sciences and demands the integration of biophysical sciences in the curriculum. The key tasks will be to build awareness of those issues among students and to provide them with tools to integrate those aspects in strategic thinking and decision-making. Business school students must create and run more resilient and inclusive business models building on a clear understanding of the natural environment in which to run operations. Integrating those aspects in the curriculum will change what business schools can promise and what students should expect.

Business schools can help organizations to build more resilient business models but the issues to be addressed will also demand public intervention. Organizations alone are unlikely to be able to address the challenges ahead. As "grand challenges" related to the Anthropocene are wicked problems with multiple causes,[10] addressing those challenges demands coordination between multiple actors, including policymakers and public authorities.[11] This eventually questions the traditional divide between political sciences and business studies to build more comprehensive approaches to address grand challenges. It also calls for business research to move beyond focusing on business practices, engage with public policy, and consider how it can address those grand challenges in a holistic manner. For example, private entities must move beyond organizational boundaries and reconsider relationships within the entire value chain. Considering these relations only from the perspective of bargaining power[12] seems obsolete when it comes to addressing the grand challenges in the Anthropocene. Businesses must take into account the impact across the value chain—from extraction, manufacturing, and distribution to consumption and disposal—and consider how coordinated efforts can reduce adverse impact on the environment. Considering the whole value chain will become increasingly mandatory as reporting initiatives and legal requirements will demand that companies exert "due diligence" and conduct audits of their value chain, report on sustainability issues, and take action to address potential problems.

We have seen throughout this book how the ecological transition forces us to rethink the role of business in shaping the economy. Education and training are key to a successful ecological transition. Business schools have the capacity to shape the understanding, behaviours, and beliefs of the future generations of responsible leaders. It is worth repeating that the situation calls for a profound questioning of what is taught, researched, and actually done in business schools. Together, with an increasing number of our peer institutions, we are actively on that path.

Hugues Bouthinon-Dumas
Arijit Chatterjee
Bernard Leca

Notes

1 Edwards, M. G., Alcaraz, J. M., & Cornell, S. E. (2021). Management education and Earth System science: Transformation as if planetary boundaries mattered. *Business & Society*, *60*, 26–56.

2 Rockström, J., Steffen, W., Noone, K., Persson, Å., Chapin, F. S., Lambin, E. F., Lenton, T. M., Scheffer, M., Folke, C., Schellnhuber, H. J., Nykvist, B., de Wit, C. A., Hughes, T., van der Leeuw, S., Rodhe, H., Sörlin, S., Snyder, P. K., Costanza, R., Svedin, U., Falkenmark, M., Karlberg, L., Corell, R. W., Fabry, V. J., Hansen, J., Walker, B., Liverman, D., Richardson, K., Crutzen, P., & Foley, J. A. (2009). A safe operating space for humanity. *Nature*, *461*(7263), 472–475.

Steffen, W., Richardson, K., Rockström, J., Cornell, S. E., Fetzer, I., Bennett, E. M., Biggs, R., Carpenter, S. R., de Vries, W., de Wit, C. A., Folke, C., Gerten, D., Heinke, J., Mace, G. M., Persson, L. M., Ramanathan, V., Reyers, B., & Sörlin, S. (2015). Planetary boundaries: Guiding human development on a changing planet. *Science*, *347*(6223), 1259855.

3 Bai, X., Bjørn, A., Kılkış, S., Muñoz, O. S., Whiteman, G., Hoff, H., Andersen, L. S., & Rockström, J. (2022). How to stop cities and companies causing planetary harm. *Nature*, *609*, 463–466.

4 OECD. (2010). *Globalization, transport and the environment*. OECD Publications. Online: https://www.oecd-ilibrary.org/environment/globalisation-transport-and-the-environment_9789264072916-en

5 Dong, F., Hu, M., Gao, Y., Liu, Y., Zhu, J., & Pan, Y. (2022). How does digital economy affect carbon emissions? Evidence from global 60 countries. *Science of the Total Environment*, *852*. http://dx.doi.org/10.1016/j.scitotenv.2022.158401.

6 International Energy Agency. (2024). *Electricity 2024: Analysis and forecast for 2026*. IEA. Online: https://www.iea.org/reports/electricity-2024

7 Chhabra, E. (2023). Working to restore: Harnessing the power of regenerative business to heal the world. Beacon Press.

8 Raworth, K. (2017). Doughnut economics: Seven ways to think like a 21st century economist. Penguin Random House.

9 Peters, K., & Thomas, H. (2023). Business schools should be schools of management: An evolutionary perspective. In E. Cornuel, H. Thomas, & M. Wood (Eds.), *Perspectives on the impact, mission and purpose of the business school*. Routledge.

10 George, G., Howard-Grenville, J., Joshi, A., & Tihanyi, L. (2016). Understanding and tackling societal grand challenges through management research. *Academy of Management Journal*, *59*, 1880–1895.

11 Chatterjee, A., Ghosh, A., & Leca, B. (2023). Double weaving: A bottom-up process of connecting locations and scales to mitigate grand challenges. *Academy of Management Journal*, *66*(3), 797–828.

Westley, F., Antadze, N., Riddell, D., Robinson, K., & Geobey, S. (2014). Five configurations for scaling up social innovation: Case examples of non-profit organizations from Canada. *Journal of Applied Behavioral Science*, *50*(3), 1–27.

12 Porter, M. (1980). *Competitive strategy*. Free Press.

Index

Note: Page numbers in *italic* indicate a figure and page numbers in **bold** indicate a table on the corresponding page.